The Complete DOD NIST 800-171 Compliance Manual

Comprehensive Controlled Unclassified Information (CUI)
Marking & Handling Section

Updated Discussion of the DOD's
Cybersecurity Maturity Model Certification (CMMC)

Mark A. Russo, CISSP-ISSAP
Former Chief Information Security Officer, Department of Education

Copyright 2020, Syber-Risk.com, All Rights Reserved
Washington, DC ∞ Tucson, AZ

DEDICATION

This book is dedicated to my supportive instructors and professors at the National Defense University, Washington, DC, and their daily efforts to train and teach the next generation of cyber-warriors of this great Nation.

This is also dedicated to my family, who have been supportive of my endeavors to plunge into writing as not just a hobby but a calling to make the world a better and more secure place.

Copyright 2020, Syber-Risk.com, All Rights Reserved
Washington, DC ∞ Tucson, AZ

The Complete DOD NIST 800-171 Compliance Manual

by Mark A. Russo

Copyright © 2020 Syber-Risk.com LLC. All rights reserved.

Printed in the United States of America.

2019:

Revision History for the First Edition

UPDATE February 2020-B with CSP Code

The Syber-Risk Logo is a registered trademark of Syber-Risk.com LLC **The Complete DOD NIST 800-171 Compliance Manual.** *While the publisher and the authors have used good faith efforts to ensure that the information and instructions contained in this work are accurate, the publisher and the authors disclaim all responsibility for errors or omissions, including without limitation responsibility for damages resulting from the use of or reliance on this work. The use of the information and instructions contained in this work is at your own risk. If any code samples or other technology this work contains or describes is subject to open source licenses or the intellectual property rights of others, it is your responsibility to ensure that your use thereof complies with such licenses or rights.*

Check Out the
<u>*Most-Extensive*</u> **Cybersecurity Blog Site**

This is the primary resource of everything, "Cyber."
"The good, the bad, and the ugly of cybersecurity all in one place."

Join us at https://cybersentinel.tech

This free resource is available to everyone interested in the fate and future of cybersecurity in the 21st Century

Copyright 2020, Syber-Risk.com, All Rights Reserved
Washington, DC ∞ Tucson, AZ

The Complete DOD NIST 800-171 Compliance Manual

Table of Contents

DOD's Cybersecurity Maturity Model Certification and NIST 800-171	18
DOD Cybersecurity IS serious	21
Pursuing an expansion of NIST-based cybersecurity standards	23
What does compliance mean for DOD?	24
Proof of a company's cybersecurity posture	25
More About Artifacts and POAMs	27
A Cybersecurity State of Mind	29
Tailoring-out Controls Possibilities	30
Proper Marking of CUI	32
CUI Banner Markings (Reference 32 CFR 2002.20(b))	33
CUI Banner Control Markings (Reference 32 CFR 2002.20(b)(1))	34
CUI Categories and Subcategories (Reference 32 CFR 2002.12)	35
Banner Markings for Category and Subcategory Markings (Reference 32 CFR 2002.20(b)(2))	37
Banner Markings with Multiple of Subcategory Markings (Reference 32 CFR 2002.20)	39
Banner Markings (Limited Dissemination Controls)(Reference 32 CFR 2002.20(b)(3)	40
Designation Indicator (Reference 32 CFR 2002.20(a)(3)(d))	41
Portion Markings (Reference 32 CFR 2002.20(f))	42
Portion Markings with Category Only (Reference 32 CFR 2002.20(f))	45
Portion Markings with Category and Dissemination Caveats (Reference 32 CFR 2002.20(f))	46
Marking of Multiple Pages (Reference 32 CFR 2002.20(c))	47
Required Indicators as directed by Authorities (Reference 32 CFR 2002.20 (b)(2)(iii))	48
Supplemental Administrative Markings (Reference 32 CFR 2002.20(l))	49
Electronic Media Storage and Marking Procedures (Reference 32 CFR 2002.20)	51
Marking Forms (Reference 32 CFR 2002.20)	52
CUI Coversheets (Reference 32 CFR 2002.32)	53

Marking Transmittal Documents (Reference 32 CFR 2002.20) 54

Alternate Marking Methods (Reference 32 CFR 2002.20) 55

Room or Area Markings (Reference 32 CFR 2002.20) 56

Container Markings (Reference 32 CFR 2002.20) 57

Shipping and Mailing (Reference 32 CFR 2002.20) 57

Re-marking Legacy Information (Reference 32 CFR 2002.36) 58

CUI MARKINGS IN A CLASSIFIED ENVIRONMENT 60

Marking Commingled Information (Reference 32 CFR 2002.20(g)) 60

Commingling Portion Markings (Reference 32 CFR 2002.20(g)) 66

Using this Book—A "How To" 68

ACCESS CONTROL (AC) 71

3.1.1 Limit information system access to authorized users, processes acting on behalf of authorized users, or devices (including other information systems). 73

3.1.2 Limit information system access to the types of transactions and functions that authorized users are permitted to execute. 75

3.1.3 Control the flow of CUI flowing the approved authorizations. 75

3.1.4 Separate the duties of individuals to reduce the risk of malevolent activity without collusion. 79

3.1.5 Employ the principle of least privilege, including for specific security functions and privileged accounts. 80

3.1.6 Use non-privileged accounts or roles when accessing nonsecurity functions. 80

3.1.7 Prevent non-privileged users from executing privileged functions and audit the execution of such functions. 81

3.1.8 Limit unsuccessful logon attempts. 83

3.1.9 Provide privacy and security notices consistent with applicable CUI rules. 84

3.1.10. Use session lock with pattern-hiding displays to prevent access/viewing of data after a period of inactivity. 86

3.1.11. Terminate (automatically) a user session after a defined condition. 87

3.1.12 Monitor and control remote access sessions. 88

3.1.13 Employ cryptographic mechanisms to protect the confidentiality of remote access sessions. 89

3.1.14 Route remote access via managed access control points 90

3.1.15 Authorize remote execution of privileged commands and remote access to security-relevant information. 91

3.1.16 Authorize wireless access prior to allowing such connections. 92

3.1.17 Protect wireless access using authentication and encryption. 93

3.1.18. Control connection of mobile devices. 94

3.1.19. Encrypt CUI on mobile devices. 95

3.1.20 Verify and control/limit connections to and use of external systems 95

3.1.21 Limit use of organizational portable storage devices on external systems. 96

3.1.22 Control CUI posted or processed on publicly accessible systems. 97

AWARENESS & TRAINING (AT) 100

3.2.1 Ensure that managers, systems administrators, and users of organizational information systems are made aware of the security risks associated with their activities and of the applicable policies, standards, and procedures related to the security of organizational information systems. 101

3.2.2 Ensure that organizational personnel are adequately trained to carry out their assigned information, security-related duties and responsibilities. 102

3.2.3 Provide security awareness training on recognizing and reporting potential indicators of insider threat 104

AUDIT AND ACCOUNTABILITY (AU) 106

3.3.1 Create, protect, and retain information system audit records to the extent needed to enable the monitoring, analysis, investigation, and reporting of unlawful, unauthorized, or inappropriate information system activity. 107

3.3.2 Ensure that the actions of individual information system users can be uniquely traced to those users, so they can be held accountable for their actions. 109

3.3.3 Review and update audited events. 110

3.3.4 Alert in the event of an audit process failure. 111

3.3.5 Correlate audit review, analysis, and reporting processes for investigation and response to indications of inappropriate, suspicious, or unusual activity. 112

3.3.6 Provide audit reduction and report generation to support on-demand analysis and reporting. 113

3.3.7 Provide an information system capability that compares and synchronizes internal system clocks with an authoritative source to generate timestamps for audit records. 113

3.3.8 Protect audit information and audit tools from unauthorized access, modification, and deletion. 114

3.3.9 Limit management of audit functionality to a subset of privileged users. 115

CONFIGURATION MANAGEMENT (CM) 117

3.4.1 Establish and maintain baseline configurations and inventories of organizational information systems (including hardware, software, firmware, and documentation) throughout the respective system development life cycles. 117

3.4.2 Establish and enforce security configuration settings for information technology products employed in organizational information systems. 119

3.4.3 Track, review, approve/disapprove, and audit changes to information systems. 119

3.4.4 Analyze the security impact of changes prior to implementation. 120

3.4.5 Define, document, approve, and enforce physical and logical access restrictions associated with changes to the information system. 121

3.4.6 Employ the principle of least functionality by configuring the information system to provide only essential capabilities. 122

3.4.7 Restrict, disable, and prevent the use of nonessential programs, functions, ports, protocols, and services. 123

3.4.8 Apply deny-by-exception (blacklist) policy to prevent the use of unauthorized software or deny all, permit-by-exception (whitelisting) policy to allow the execution of authorized software. 125

IDENTIFICATION AND AUTHENTICATION (IA) 128

3.5.1 Identify information system users, processes acting on behalf of users, or devices. 129

3.5.2 Authenticate (or verify) the identities of those users, processes, or devices, as a prerequisite to allowing access to organizational information systems. 129

3.5.3 Use multifactor authentication for local and network access to privileged accounts and for network access to non-privileged accounts. 131

3.5.4 Employ replay-resistant authentication mechanisms for network access to privileged and nonprivileged accounts. 131

3.5.5 Prevent reuse of identifiers for a defined period. 132

3.5.6 Disable identifiers after a defined period of inactivity. 133

3.5.7 Enforce a minimum password complexity and change of characters when new passwords are created. 133

3.5.8 Prohibit password reuse for a specified number of generations. 135

3.5.9 Allow temporary password use for system logons with an immediate change to a permanent password. 135

3.5.10 Store and transmit only encrypted representation of passwords. 135

3.5.11. Obscure feedback of authentication information. 136

INCIDENT RESPONSE (IR) 137

3.6.1 Establish an operational incident-handling capability for organizational information systems that includes adequate preparation, detection, analysis, containment, recovery, and user response activities. 139

3.6.2 Track, document, and report incidents to appropriate officials and/or authorities both internal and external to the organization. 142

3.6.3 Test the organizational incident response capability. 142

MAINTENANCE (MA) 144

3.7.1 Perform maintenance on organizational information systems. 144

3.7.2 Provide effective controls on the tools, techniques, mechanisms, and personnel used to conduct information system maintenance. 144

3.7.3 Ensure equipment removed for off-site maintenance is sanitized of any CUI. 145

3.7.4 Check media containing diagnostic and test programs for malicious code before the media are used in the information system. 146

3.7.5 Require multifactor authentication to establish nonlocal maintenance sessions via external network connections and terminate such connections when nonlocal maintenance is complete. 146

3.7.6 Supervise the maintenance activities of maintenance personnel without required access authorization. 147

MEDIA PROTECTION (MP) 148

3.8.1 Protect (i.e., physically control and securely store) information system media containing CUI, both paper and digital. 149

3.8.2 Limit access to CUI on information system media to authorized users. 150

3.8.3 Sanitize or destroy information system media containing CUI before disposal or release for reuse. 150

3.8.4 Mark media with necessary CUI markings and distribution limitations. 155

3.8.5 Control access to media containing CUI and maintain accountability for media during transport outside of controlled areas. 156

3.8.6 Implement cryptographic mechanisms to protect the confidentiality of CUI stored on digital media during transport unless otherwise protected by alternative physical safeguards. 157

3.8.7 Control the use of removable media on information system components. 157

3.8.8 Prohibit the use of portable storage devices when such devices have no identifiable owner. 158

3.8.9 Protect the confidentiality of backup CUI at storage locations. 158

PERSONNEL SECURITY (PS) 159

3.9.1 Screen individuals prior to authorizing access to information systems containing CUI. 159

3.9.2 Ensure that CUI and information systems containing CUI are protected during and after personnel actions such as terminations and transfers. 160

PHYSICAL PROTECTION (PP) 161

3.10.1 Limit physical access to organizational information systems, equipment, and the respective operating environments to authorized individuals. 161

3.10.2 Protect and monitor the physical facility and support infrastructure for those information systems. 162

3.10.3 Escort visitors and monitor visitor activity. 163

3.10.4 Maintain audit logs of physical access. 164

3.10.5 Control and manage physical access devices. 164

3.10.6 Enforce safeguarding measures for CUI at alternate worksites (e.g., telework sites). 165

RISK ASSESSMENT (RA) 167

3.11.1 Periodically assess the risk to organizational operations (including mission, functions, image, or reputation), organizational assets, and individuals, resulting from the operation of organizational information systems and the associated processing, storage, or transmission of CUI. 169

3.11.2 Scan for vulnerabilities in the information system and applications periodically and when new vulnerabilities affecting the system are identified. 170

3.11.3 Remediate vulnerabilities in accordance with assessments of risk. 172

SECURITY ASSESSMENT (SA) 173

3.12.1 Periodically assess the security controls in organizational information systems to determine if the controls are effective in their application. 173

3.12.2 Develop and implement plans of action designed to correct deficiencies and reduce or eliminate vulnerabilities in organizational information systems. 174

3.12.3 Monitor information system security controls on an ongoing basis to ensure the continued effectiveness of the controls. 175

3.12.4   Develop, document, and periodically update system security plans that describe system boundaries, system environments of operation, how security requirements are implemented, and the relationships with or connections to other systems. 176

SYSTEM AND COMMUNICATIONS PROTECTION (SC) 178

3.13.1 Monitor, control, and protect organizational communications (i.e., information transmitted or received by organizational information systems) at the external boundaries and key internal boundaries of the information systems. 178

3.13.2 Employ architectural designs, software development techniques, and systems engineering principles that promote effective information security within organizational information systems. 180

3.13.3 Separate user functionality from information system management functionality. 181

3.13.4 Prevent unauthorized and unintended information transfer via shared system resources. 182

3.13.5 Implement subnetworks for publicly accessible system components that are physically or logically separated from internal networks 183

3.13.6 Deny network communications traffic by default and allow network communications traffic by exception (i.e., deny all, permit by exception). ... 183

3.13.7 Prevent remote devices from simultaneously establishing non-remote connections with the information system and communicating via some other connection to resources in external networks. ... 184

3.13.8 Implement cryptographic mechanisms to prevent unauthorized disclosure of CUI during transmission unless otherwise protected by alternative physical safeguards. ... 184

3.13.9 Terminate network connections associated with communications sessions at the end of the sessions or after a defined period of inactivity. ... 185

3.13.10 Establish and manage cryptographic keys for cryptography employed in the information system. ... 186

3.13.11 Employ FIPS-validated cryptography when used to protect the confidentiality of CUI ... 189

3.13.12 Prohibit remote activation of collaborative computing devices and provide indication of devices in use to users present at the device. ... 190

3.13.13 Control and monitor the use of mobile code. ... 191

3.13.14 Control and monitor the use of Voice over Internet Protocol (VoIP) technologies. ... 192

3.13.15 Protect the authenticity of communications sessions. ... 192

3.13.16 Protect the confidentiality of CUI at rest. ... 193

SYSTEM AND INFORMATION INTEGRITY (SI) ... 194

3.14.1 Identify, report, and correct information and information system flaws in a timely manner. ... 194

3.14.2 Provide protection from malicious code at appropriate locations within organizational information systems. ... 196

3.14.3 Monitor information system security alerts and advisories and take appropriate actions in response. ... 199

3.14.4 Update malicious code protection mechanisms when new releases are available. ... 200

3.14.5 Perform periodic scans of the information system and real-time scans of files from external sources as files are downloaded, opened, or executed. ... 200

3.14.6 Monitor the information system including inbound and outbound communications traffic, to detect attacks and indicators of potential attacks. ... 202

3.14.7 Identify unauthorized use of the information system. ... 202

MATURITY IS A MATTER OF CONTROL IMPLEMENTATION ... 204

APPENDIX A -- RELEVANT REFERENCES ... 206

APPENDIX B -- TERMS & GLOSSARY ... 207

APPENDIX C – CONTINUOUS MONITORING: *A More Detailed Discussion* ... 212

APPENDIX D – NIST 800-171 COMPLIANCE CHECKLIST ... 227

- Access Control (AC) 227
- Awareness & Training (AT) 233
- Audit & Accountability (AU) 235
- Configuration Management (CM) 238
- Identification & Authentication (IA) 242
- Incident Response (IR) 245
- Maintenance (MA) 247
- Media Protection (MP) 249
- Personnel Security (PS) 251
- Physical Security (PP) 252
- Risk Assessments (RA) 254
- Security Assessments (SA) 256
- System & Communications Protection (SC) 258
- System & Information Integrity (SI) 263

ABOUT THE AUTHOR 265

DOD's Cybersecurity Maturity Model Certification and NIST 800-171

In 2019, the Department of Defense (DoD) announced the development of the **Cybersecurity Maturity Model Certification** (CMMC). The CMMC is a framework *not unlike* NIST 800-171; however, it is a duplicate effort to the National Institute of Standards and Technology (NIST) 800-171 with **ONE** significant difference. CMMC is nothing more than an evolution of NIST 800-171, with elements from NIST 800-53 and ISO 27001, that includes and directs **third-party auditing** by cybersecurity professionals recognized by the DOD. In addition to assessing the maturity of a company's implementation of cybersecurity controls, the CMMC will also evaluate the company's maturity/ institutionalization of cybersecurity practices and processes. The security controls and methodologies will be the same—the DOD still has no recognition of this apparent duplication.[1]

> **Companies will be certified at the appropriate CMMC level based upon the sensitivity of the system and its data. CMMC also affects sub-contractors that will also be required to meet CMMC requirements**

The DOD will require third-party assessment of a company's Information Technology (IT) system and data protection measures using the same NIST controls as based upon the foundational federal NIST framework, as found in NIST 800-53 revision 4 (with revision 5 pending). The DOD's efforts will also include establishing a contract agency that will act as the "authorizing official" (AO) on behalf of the federal government. Current contract Requests for Information and Proposals are not expected to be completed until late 2020. Furthermore, CMMC is initially only focused at DOD's Defense Industrial Base (DIB) partners and is specific to Controlled Unclassified Information (CUI), and not national security designation information or data.

---

[1] The author has over a decade working with NIST 800-53 and 800-171, respectively. Unfortunately, this is a key problem of RMF in that senior leadership lacks the depth and understanding of the application of RMF, vis-à-vis 800-53 and 800-171.

NIST 800-171 allowed for self-assessment by contractors, and the CMMC does not permit this current **weakness** of NIST 800-171. It recognizes that the technical capabilities of the defense contracting community have been less than complete. When it comes to an understanding of the Risk Management Framework (RMF), CMMC is a result of historically poor cybersecurity contracting management and oversight that has plagued the DOD as well as the entirety of the federal government for years.

Contractors **will** be required to be certified by a third-party auditor. There has been no guidance to-date of what certification a CMMC audit company must have—*who is auditing the auditors?* Defense Contract Management Agency (DCMA) and the Defense Counterintelligence and Security Agency (DCSA) will have purview over the CMMC, but neither have the current capabilities nor experience to execute the CMMC framework.

The Council of Economic Advisers, an agency within the Executive Office of the President, estimates that malicious cyber activity cost the U.S. economy between $57 billion and $109 Billion in 2016
[Source: The Cost of Malicious Cyber Activity to the U.S. Economy, CEA, 2018]

An organization will directly coordinate with an accredited and independent third-party commercial certification organization as designated by the DOD. Organizations company will select the certification level as either high (for sensitive DOD systems) through low (basic systems) per NIST guidance 800-53 and 800-37, Guide for Applying the Risk Management Framework to Federal Information Systems: A Security Life Cycle Approach, Revision 1, dated June 5, 2014

Companies will be certified at the appropriate CMMC level based upon the sensitivity of the system and its data. CMMC also affects sub-contractors that will also be required to meet CMMC requirements.

The CMMC framework arose in response to the many extreme breaches of DOD information and weapon systems to include, for example, the F-35, Joint Strike Fighter (JSF) program, where direct connections with Chinese cybersecurity operations against the US has been highly successful. DOD's current reliance on the security controls in NIST 800-171 that does not require third-party assessment, was presumed enough to thwart the increasing and evolving threat; however, that has proved a poor decision by the DOD.

CMMC is expected to include portions of various cybersecurity standards, such as NIST 800-171, ISO 270001, and ISO 27032; however, at its core, NIST 800-53 is the universally accepted standard for DOD systems. NIST 800-53 will provide the basis of any standards of best security practices and a measure of the "maturity of a company's institutionalization of cybersecurity practices and processes."

The cost of certification will become allowable as a reimbursable cost of typical contract negotiations under the Federal Acquisition Regulation (FAR), and more specifically, under the Defense Federal Acquisition Regulation Supplement (DFARS). While the current guidance states that the costs "will not be prohibitive," the DOD has yet to identify specified tasks and activities required to conduct auditing by third-party organizations that meet the CMMC "standard."

For additional and updated information, it is best to continually check the Office of the Under Secretary of Defense for Acquisition and Sustainment website at https://www.acq.osd.mil/cmmc/index.html. **The DOD** is planning to release Version 1.0 of CMMC by January 2020; however, expect it to be delayed is as typical to these extensive—but critical—efforts by the DOD. Contractors are expected to include CMMC costs in future proposals by June 2020; however, expect that to be delayed more likely into 2021-2022 timeframes.

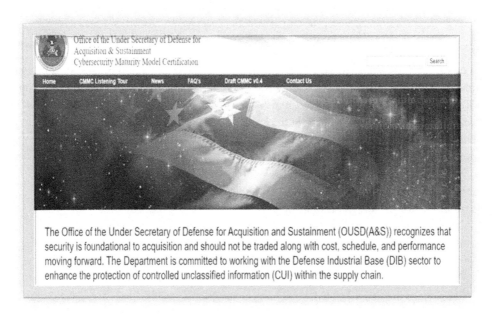

DOD Cybersecurity IS serious

This book is created to help the small and big business owner in meeting the newest in cybersecurity contracting requirements to conduct business with the Department of Defense (DOD). It is intended to assist companies, and their Information Technology (IT) staffs' on how to best address the DOD challenges of meeting the demands of the 2016 National Institute of Standards and Technology (NIST) Special Publication (SP) 800-171, revision 1, *Protecting Controlled Unclassified Information in Nonfederal Information Systems and Organizations.* This includes compliance with the Federal Acquisition Regulation (FAR) clause 52.204-21 and its companion DOD supplement, the Defense Federal Acquisition Regulation Supplement (DFARS), and its specific clause, 252.204-7012.

To participate in any current or future DOD contract effort, either as a prime or subcontractor, a company is REQUIRED to be fully NIST 800-171 revision 1 compliant. As of December 31, 2017, any company wishing to do business with DOD is required to meet the **110** NIST-based security controls.[2] Companies can implement these security solutions either directly or by using outside, third-party, "managed services" to satisfy the protection requirements of Controlled Unclassified Information (CUI)/Covered Defense Information (CDI)[3] NIST publications while not previously mandatory for "nonfederal entities," NIST 800-171 rev. 1, is the first time that a federal agency has mandated nonfederal agencies, vis a vis, private companies, comply with this federal-specific publication. "Nonfederal" organizations, such as businesses, and their internal IT systems processing, storing, or transmitting CUI may be required to comply with this publication. In the case of DOD, that suggestion is *now* mandatory.

The requirement to protect information and data is not just limited to the financial services, insurance, and health care sectors. It is hard to identify a federal or industrial sector that escapes some responsibility to protect its electronic data. Indeed, some areas deal with more sensitive information, so it is not a surprise that the Department of Defense (DoD) recently took steps to have its contractors provide "adequate security" for "covered defense information (CDI)," which includes Controlled Unclassified Information (CUI).

To further emphasize to those future companies wishing to conduct business with the DOD, they have issued guidance that requires such companies to demonstrate DOD's insistence on strong cybersecurity practices from its third-party providers and its intent to eliminate its business connections with those who do not conform with this mandate. This guidance is destined to be a model for other federal agencies and industries to place similar pressures on those vendors to include the rest of the federal executive branches to include,

---

[2] Compliance between the CMMC and NIST 800-171 will likely be a long and ambiguous discussion for the next few years; however, following NIST 800-171 and identifying third-party auditors to support any federal compliance efforts is the better course of action as of the publication of this book.

[3] The Term CDI no longer exists under the current implementation of the CMMC. It is only provided here for potential application as the CMMC evolves over the next several years (the author).

for example, the Department of Homeland Security (DHS), the Department of Commerce (DOC), and Veterans Administration (VA); expect those changes to happen shortly from the federal government and to have a much broader impact at a national level.

This mandate currently exists in the form of *Defense Federal Acquisition Regulation Supplement* (DFARS) clause 252.204-7012. This regulation is construed in conjunction with the NIST 800-171 revision 1, that direct 110 security controls to measure whether a company provides "adequate security" to its IT infrastructure "connected" to the DOD's systems, its data stores, and databases.

Since December 31, 2017, a company that fails to have "adequate security" risks losing its contracts and ability to sell to the DoD. As a result, government contractors have come under more significant pressure and scrutiny to comply with NIST 800-171. Subcontractors face the same, if not higher, pressures as part of the global supply chain connection between the direct supplier and the DOD.

The new guidance, "DoD Guidance for Reviewing System Security Plans and the NIST SP 800-171 Security Requirements Not Yet Implemented," was recently issued by NIST. The guidance is characterized as a tool to help the DoD and contractors assess their System Security Plans (SSPs) and Plans of Action (POAs) and to prioritize what steps should be undertaken to satisfy the DFARS 252.204-7012 mandate for "adequate security."

NIST SP 800-171, "Protecting Controlled Unclassified Information in Nonfederal Systems and Organizations," establishes the 110 controls to adequately protect sensitive data that is exchanged between the business and the DOD. These controls are used to measure whether a contractor has established an adequate cybersecurity program to meet the requirements of the new DOD regulation. The guidance identifies *NIST-assigned priority codes (P1-P5) and "DoD Value" ranges (5-1) to each of these controls*. These values should help measure contractor SSPs and POAs as part of a Request for Proposal (RFP), as well as the impact of those NIST SP 800-171 security requirements that have not yet been implemented to a contractor's overall cybersecurity program.

This DoD guidance also addresses methods by which the security requirements that have not been met may be implemented and, when applicable, the direction provides additional clarification to the company or business. Methods of implementation may include reconfiguration of the IT system, the procurement of hardware and software, or the development of written corporate policies and procedures. This guidance will better enable DOD and Nonfederal Organization (NFO), specifically businesses, to better prioritize and address any gaps in their cybersecurity program in the context of the NIST 800-171 standard, and to deploy appropriate information security controls in a more structured and efficient manner.

The new direction also provides government personnel and its contractors' further objective criteria to measure whether a third-party provider, to include the growing Cloud Service Provider (CSP) community, acceptable cybersecurity program that will protect the confidentiality, integrity, and availability of its respective stores of CUI/CDI. The guidance further demonstrates which businesses have implemented a holistic cybersecurity program and those who have not to the DOD and beyond.

It is unlikely to long term that this narrow implementation of the NIST 800-171 assessment approach will be limited to the DoD, its contractors, and their subcontractors. Third-party vendor, external service provider, management is a vital constituent of any well-developed cybersecurity program. For instance, under 23 NYCRR 500.11, the New York cyber regulations will soon require "Covered Entities" to implement written policies and procedures to conduct due diligence of the cybersecurity posture of their business or company. The expansion of such frameworks is expected to not only expand beyond the DOD and the remaining federal executive agencies but state and local municipalities as soon as the emphasis and direction grow over the next years.

Pursuing an expansion of NIST-based cybersecurity standards

Ongoing intrusions into critical federal systems point to the ever agile and highly impactful effects of cyber-threats worldwide. Reports of the large volumes of personal data exfiltrated from the Office of Personnel Management (OPM), and intrusions into seemingly highly protected networks of the DOD, highlights the need for change. "For nearly a week, some 4,000-key military and civilian personnel working for the Joint Chiefs of Staff [had] lost access to their unclassified email after what is now believed to be an intrusion into the critical Pentagon server that handles that email network..." (Starr, B., 2015, July 31. The military is still dealing with cyber-attack 'mess.' Retrieved from CNN.com: http://www.cnn.com/2015/07/31/politics/defense-department-computer-intrusion-email-server/)

The need to implement and enhance the Risk Management Framework (RMF) based on NIST's cybersecurity-focused 800-series continues to be highly debated. The challenge has been about whether to expand the NIST RMF "framework" beyond the federal government's multiple IT security boundaries. What if the federal government mandated its applicability to the private sector? Can the expansion of the NIST 800-series, to include specifically NIST 800-171, provide a better means to protect the Nation's sensitive data?

This also includes enhancing laws and regulations to increase corporate and business cybersecurity protections; this comprises current legislation such as the Federal Information Security Management Act (FISMA) of 2002 and updated by Congress in 2014. These laws, regulations, and processes will hopefully improve and protect the critical infrastructures and sensitive data stored within the physical boundaries of the US and its vital corporations. Presumably, such an evolution will better protect the US's vital and sensitive data from both internal and foreign state actors desiring to harm the US.

FISMA was written by Congress to reduce the effectiveness of cyber-attacks against the federal government and its vast IT infrastructure. FISMA and other cybersecurity laws provide a needed method to enhance oversight of information security applications, systems, and networks. FISMA further explicitly sought to "...provide a comprehensive framework for ensuring the effectiveness of information security controls over information resources that support Federal operations and assets" (US Government. (2002). Federal Information Security Management Act of 2002 (44 U.S.C. §§ 3541-3549). Retrieved from NIST: http://csrc.nist.gov/drivers/documents/FISMA-final.pdf)).

In 2014, DOD internally adopted the NIST RMF 800-series as the standard. The overall effort has become the current DOD direction and guidance to more effectively protect its own critical IT infrastructure, and to expand beyond its boundaries to protect *its* data transmitted into the private sector.

NIST 800-171 rev. 1 is the first attempt for DOD that applies to vendors and contractors to ensure CUI/CDI is appropriately protected from threats. It is further mandated that information about a company's business specific to the DOD is protected from compromise or exploit; that is a modification, loss, or destruction. DOD is attempting to ensure an essential effort is executed to protect the company's own internal CUI as well as co-mingled DOD information that is created as part of the company's regular business operations.

What does compliance mean for DOD?

This book describes both the methods and means to "self-assess"[4] and provide requisite proof. An example is giving evidence that the Contracting Officer or designated representative of a company meets these requirements. There are **110** explicit security controls from NIST 800-171 extracted from NIST's core cybersecurity document, NIST 800-53, Security and Privacy Controls for Federal Information Systems and Organizations, which are considered vital. This is a highly pared-down set of controls to meet that requirement based on over a thousand potential controls offered from NIST 800-53 revision 4. This more expansive set of controls is used by DOD to protect all DOD systems from its jet fighters to its vast personnel databases.

This book is intended to focus business owners and their IT support staff on the minimum and more complete suggested answers to each of these controls. Companies fortunately only need to focus on how to best address these "minimal" controls to the government—and, it more thoughtfully will help the business protect its sensitive data and Intellectual Property (IP).

The **People, Process, and Technology (PPT) Model** is the recommended guidance for answering many of the controls within NIST 800-171. While all solutions will not necessarily require a **technological** answer, consideration of the **people** (e.g., who? what skill sets? etc.) and **process** (e.g., notifications to senior management, action workflows, etc.) will meet many of the response requirements. Refer to Control 3.6.1 that provides example questions that could be offered and answered when using the People-Process-Technology (PPT) model. The best responses will typically include the types and kinds of people assigned to oversee the control, the process or procedures that identify the workflow that will ensure that the control is met, and in many cases, the technology that will answer the control in part or in full.

---

[4] As noted in the opening chapter, self-assessment is not going to be allowed by the DOD under the CMMC framework. Contractors SHOULD always conduct an internal self-assessment in order to reduce costs and develop an understanding of the NIST 800-171 and 53 security requirements.

PPT Model

Proof of a company's cybersecurity posture

The basis of NIST 800-171 is that contractors provide adequate security on all covered contractor Information Systems (IS). Typically, the minimum requirement to demonstrate control implementation is through documentation. Another term that is used throughout this book is an artifact. An artifact is any representation to an independent third-party assessor that shows compliance with specific security control. It is a significant part of the proof that a business owner would provide DOD.

The common term for the collection of all applications and supporting artifacts is the Body of Evidence (BOE). The critical items required for the BOE includes three major elements:

1. **Company Policy or Procedure.** For this book, these terms are used interchangeably. Substantially any direction provided to internal employees and subcontractors that are enforceable under United States (US) labor laws and Human Resource (HR) direction. It is recommended that such a policy or procedure artifact be a unique collection of how the company addresses each of the 110 security controls.

> *All policy or procedure requirements are best captured in a single business policy or procedure guide. This should address the controls aligned with the security control families*

2. **System Security Plan (SSP).** This is a standard cybersecurity document. It describes the company's overall IT infrastructure to include hardware and software lists. Where appropriate, suggestions of additional artifacts that should be included in this document and duplicated into a DOD standard SSP format will be recommended. (See *System Security Plan (SSP) Template and Workbook: A Supplement to Understanding Your Responsibility to Meet NIST 800-171* on Amazon®)

   A *free* 36-minute introduction to the SSP is currently available on Udemy.com at https://www.udemy.com/system-security-plan-ssp-for-nist-800-171-compliance/.

3. **Plans of Action and Milestones (POAM).** This describes any control that the company cannot fix or fully demonstrate its full compliance with the control. It provides an opportunity for a company to delay addressing a difficult to implement a technical solution or because the cost may be prohibitive.

   POAMs should always have an expected completion date and defined interim milestones (typically monthly) that describes the actions leading to a full resolution or implementation of the control. ***POAMs usually should not be for*** *more than a year; however, a critical hint, a company can request an <u>extension</u> multiple times if unable to fully meet the control.*

 When working with the government, being simple and consistent always help through a very young and undefined process

More About Artifacts and POAMs

Other artifacts that will are suggested including screen captures. All current Operating Systems (OS) includes a "print screen" function where the text or image is captured, placed in temporary computer memory, and can be easily inserted into other locations or hard copy printed. IT personnel should use this function to show, for example, policy settings and system logging (audit) data. When in doubt, always have some form of graphical representation to show the government.

The POAM will be used where the business cannot meet or address the control either for technical reasons, "we do not have a Data at Rest (DAR) encryption program," or cost, "we plan to purchase the DAR solution No Later Than April 1, 2019." POAMs should include milestones; milestones should describe what will be accomplished overtime to prepare for the full implementation of the control in the future. What will the business do in the interim to address the control? This could include, for example, other mitigation responses of using improved physical security controls, such as a 24-7 guard force, the addition of a steel-door to prevent entry to the main computer servers or improved and enforceable policies that have explicit repercussions upon personnel.

POAMs will always have a defined end date. Typically, it is either within 90 days, six months, or a year in length. For DOD, one year should be the maximum date; however, the business, as part of this fledgling process, can request an extension to the POAM past the "planned" end date. RMF affords such flexibilities; do not be afraid to exercise them as appropriate. (See Access Control (AC) for a sample template).

A Cybersecurity State of Mind

The focus is to provide the mental approach and technical understanding of what the control is (and what it is not). The first paragraph describes a MINIMUM ANSWER. This is what is needed to prepare a base answer for a minimal and acceptable level of response. Mainly, the solutions here require policy or procedural documents that describe to the government how the business will ensure this control will be met; if just trying to get through the process expeditiously, this paragraph will be enough to secure an approval.

If there is a greater desire to understand the process further and demonstrate a more substantial solution, the paragraph, MORE COMPLETE ANSWER, is designed to provide more depth. It is intended to more completely describe to the business owner how to better show an understanding to DOD its implementation of NIST 800-171.

Also, for clarification, the **Basic Security Requirement heading** is what is typically described as the **Common Control** for the control family. It is best to understand it is the primary control for the respective control family (see the **NIST 800-171 SECURITY REQUIREMENT FAMILIES**). The *Derived Security Requirements* can be considered more as supplemental and "more granular" requirements for the "parent" control. Depending on the types and kinds of data stored, these controls in the more *classic* NIST 800-53 publication can include hundreds of other controls; DOD has fortunately deemed only 110 controls as necessary.

FAMILY	FAMILY
(AC) Access Control	(MP) Media Protection
(AT) Awareness and Training	(PS) Personnel Security
(AU) Audit and Accountability	(PP) Physical Protection
(CM) Configuration Management	(RA) Risk Assessment
(IA) Identification and Authentication	(SA) Security Assessment
(IR) Incident Response	(SC) System and Communications Protection
(MA) Maintenance	(SI) System and Information Integrity

NIST 800-171 SECURITY REQUIREMENT FAMILIES

Tailoring-out Controls Possibilities

The 2016 version update to NIST 800-171, revision 1, provides an *inadequate* direction on the matter of **control tailoring**. It states in Appendix E that there are three primary criteria for the removal of security control (or control enhancement):

- **The control is uniquely federal (i.e., primarily the responsibility of the federal government):** DOD directly provides the control to the company. While possible, expect this not typically to occur.
- **The control is not directly related to protecting the confidentiality of CUI/CDI:** This will also not apply since all these controls were initially chosen to safeguard the confidentiality of all CUI/CDI. That is why this book exists to explain better how to address these controls, which are, for the most part, all required.
- **The control is expected to be routinely satisfied by Nonfederal Organizations (NFO) without specification:** In other words, the control is expected to be met by the NFO, i.e., the company (you and your IT team.)

Tailoring is wholly allowed and recommended where appropriate. Within the NIST cybersecurity framework, the concept of **tailoring-out** of a control is desirable, where technically or operationally, it cannot be reasonably applied. This will require technical certainty that the control is Non-Applicable (N/A). Under this opportunity, if the company's IT architecture does not contain within its **security boundary,** the technology where such a control would be required to be applied when the control is identified as N/A.

For example, where the business has no Wi-Fi network in its security boundary, it can advise the government that any controls addressing the security of its Wi-Fi would be an N/A control. The business cannot nor have reason to implement this control because it currently does not allow Wi-Fi networks or any presence of such equipment such as Wi-Fi routers, antennas, etc. The control would be marked as **compliant** and annotated as N/A at the time of the self-assessment. It would still be required to identify that Wi-fi is not currently authorized in the company's cybersecurity procedure guide or policy.

 Tailoring-out can be your friend

100% OFF BONUS DOWNLOAD

To show my appreciation to all my readers of specific NIST 800-171 books, I am providing FREE ACCESS to an over 250-page starter Cybersecurity Policy(CSP) template **worth over $500** for buying this book. Over three months of effort to provide you all with an 80% solution to the CSP, SSP, and other required cyber-documents. I would like to thank you all for your questions and comments to create even better resources for my fellow cybersecurity professionals around the US and around the world.

THE 100% OFF CODE IS: AMMV4Y86

Go to https://cybersentinel.tech/product/a-security-authorization-development-package-model-sadp-m-template-for-nist-800-171-accreditation-packages/

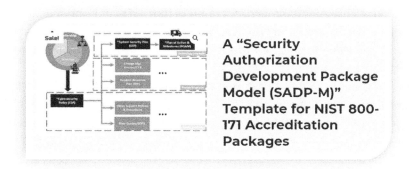

Proper Marking of CUI[5]

Security markings and safeguarding is a significant part of being successful in the application of NIST 800-171. Proper marking is not just for the company or agency, but for those not intended or authorized to view CUI. This chapter delineates how to mark all forms of written and electronic media to protect sensitive CUI. While it is unlikely a company or business will create CUI, it will be responsible for the legal protections from either administrative, civil, or criminal implications of failing to care for CUI properly. **Do not be careless.**

The CUI Program standardizes how the Executive branch handles unclassified information[6] that does not meet the criteria required for classification under E.O. 13526, "Classified National Security Information," December 29, 2009, or the Atomic Energy Act but must be protected based on law, regulation, or Government-wide policy. Protections involve the safeguards employed while this information is stored or handled by the Executive branch departments or its subordinate agencies.

Before implementation of the CUI Program, agencies employed *ad hoc*, agency-specific policies, procedures, and markings to safeguard and control this information. This information involved privacy, security, proprietary business interests, and law enforcement information. This was highly inefficient and confusing. Subsequent guidance resulted in inconsistent marking and safeguarding of documents that led to unclear or unnecessarily restrictive dissemination policies. Furthermore, it created obstacles to the *best practice* principle of *Information Sharing,* resulting in part from the 9-11 attack of September 11, 2001[7].

Proper markings alert information holders to the presence of CUI and subsequently when portion markings are required. Markings ensure that CUI is identified, and the exact information is appropriately marked for protection. They

---

[5] This chapter is adapted from the National Archives and Records Administration (NARA) information and artifacts regarding the national CUI program.

[6] While the Legislative and Judicial Branch should defer to the Executive Branch for all matters regarding national security protections and markings, it cannot be guaranteed for vendors working with the other two branches of the US government.

[7] One of the major findings of the 9-11 Commission was that the Central Intelligence Agency (CIA) and the Federal Bureau of Investigation (FBI) each had pieces of critical intelligence that may have prevented the attacks. Congress mandated created information sharing efforts—however, the parochial nature of government has not as of yet solved this problem.

alert CUI holders to any dissemination and safeguarding controls. This chapter provides basic marking guidelines for CUI and is written to give visibility and requisite security to CUI.

Companies, businesses, organizations, agencies, and most specifically, employees must review their organizations' CUI policy before marking any CUI. The handling of CUI must be per **E.O. 13556, "Controlled Unclassified Information," November 4, 2010**, 32 CFR Part 2002 (this link provides a full version https://www.govinfo.gov/content/pkg/CFR-2017-title32-vol6/pdf/CFR-2017-title32-vol6-part2002.pdf), supplemental guidance published by the government's overall CUI Executive Agent (EA), the National Archive and Records Administration (NARA), and all applicable EA-approved agency policies. This chapter contains guidance on what each marking is, where and how to apply it, and which items are mandatory or optional based on local agency or organization policy.

CUI Banner Markings (Reference 32 CFR 2002.20(b))

Banner markings are the necessary header (and footer) designations alerting individuals with a need-to-know the required restrictions in place to ensure the protection of the information. Banner makings should be seen by individuals to provide the maximum protection if the information is set out in the open or inadvertently visible to unauthorized individuals. Those individuals charged with the protection of the CUI are administratively responsible for CUI and protection and are subject to disciplinary actions by the agency or company. The following is a list of basic knowledge required by the agency as well as recipient vendors and contractors of the US Government.

- The initial marking for all CUI is the CUI Banner Marking. This is the central marking that appears at the top (and typically, at the bottom) of each page of any document that contains CUI.

- This marking is MANDATORY for all documents containing CUI. The content of the CUI Banner Marking must be inclusive of all CUI within the document and must be the same on each page.

- The Banner Marking should appear as bold capitalized black text and be centered when feasible. (*There are no designated size or font requirements, but we recommend the same font used for the document, and at least four sizes larger for visual prominence).*

- The CUI Banner Marking may include up to three elements:
    1. The CUI Control Marking (mandatory) may consist of either the word "CONTROLLED" or the acronym "CUI."
    2. CUI Category or Subcategory Markings (mandatory for CUI Specified). These are separated from the CUI Control Marking by a double forward-slash (//). When including multiple categories or subcategories in a Banner Marking, they must be alphabetized and are separated by a single forward-slash (/).
    3. Limited Dissemination (LIMDIS) Control Markings are preceded by a double forward-slash (//) to separate them from the rest of the CUI Banner Marking.

    A sample of the CUI Banner Marking may be found below.

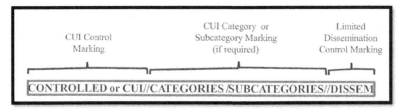

CUI Banner Marking

The above example uses the words "CATEGORIES" and "SUBCATEGORIES" as substitutes for CUI Category or Subcategory Markings and the word "DISSEM" as a substitute for Limited Dissemination Control Marking. Consult the CUI Registry for actual CUI markings.

CUI Banner Control Markings (Reference 32 CFR 2002.20(b)(1))

The CUI Control Marking is mandatory for all CUI and may consist of either the word "CONTROLLED" or the acronym "CUI" (at the designator's discretion). A best practice for CUI Banner Marking includes it being placed at the bottom of the document. Below are two examples showing the options for the CUI Banner Marking.

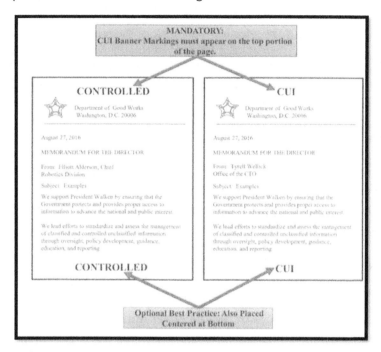

CUI Categories and Subcategories (Reference 32 CFR 2002.12)

The CUI Program is founded on the precondition that only information requiring protection based on law, Federal regulation, or government-wide policy can qualify as CUI. *CUI Categories and Subcategories are necessarily different*. CUI Categories and Subcategories are based on at least one or more laws, regulations, or government-wide policies; these are also referred to as *Authorities*[8] that require a specific type of information to be protected or restricted in its dissemination.

There are two types of CUI Categories and Subcategories: CUI Basic and CUI Specified.

---

[8] Consider Authorities as local rules or policies that are unique to the particular Federal agency. Typically, the Contract Officer should be able to assist in information briefings with the agency to ensure full compliance by the vendor.

1. ***CUI Basic*** is the standard CUI category. All rules of CUI apply to CUI Basic Categories and Subcategories. This ensures the proper creation and handling of properly marked CUI.

2. ***CUI Specified*** is different since the requirements for how users must treat each type of information vary with each Category or Subcategory. This is because some Authorities have specialized needs for handling varied kinds of CUI information.

CUI Specified is NOT a "higher level" of CUI, it is *merely different.* Also, its differences are dictated by law, Federal regulation, or government-wide policy; they cannot be ignored. Furthermore, a document containing multiple CUI Specified Categories and Subcategories must include all of them in the CUI Banner Marking.

There is one additional issue with CUI Specified. Some CUI Categories and Subcategories are only CUI Specified, sometimes based upon the Authorities' local rules or policies. The reason these differences are caused by differing laws or regulations about the same information type; however, only *some* of them may include additional or alternate handling requirements for standard CUI Basic.

Therefore, only CUI created under Authorities would be CUI Specified. Explicitly, if the law, regulation, or Government-wide policy that pertains to an agency are listed in the CUI Registry as a Specified Authority, then you must mark the CUI based on that Authority as CUI Specified and include that marking in the CUI Banner.

The CUI Registry may be found at https://www.archives.gov/cui/registry/category-list

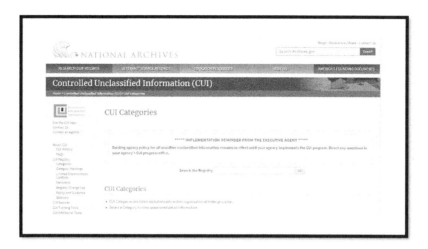

Banner Markings for Category and Subcategory Markings (Reference 32 CFR 2002.20(b)(2))

CUI Category or Subcategory Markings are separated by a double forward-slash (//) from the CUI Control Marking. When including multiple CUI Category or Subcategory Markings in the CUI Banner Marking, they must be separated by a single forward-slash (/). When a document contains CUI Specified, all CUI Specified Category or Subcategory Markings must be included in the CUI Banner Marking.

Additionally, agency heads may approve the use of CUI Basic Category or Subcategory Markings through agency CUI policy. When such agency policy exists, all CUI Basic Category or Subcategory Markings must be included in the CUI Banner Marking.

Varied Banner Markings

The above examples use the words "SP-SPECIFIED" and "BASIC" as substitutes for CUI Category and Subcategory Markings. Consult the CUI Registry for actual CUI markings.

Since CUI Specified Categories and Subcategories are different – both from CUI Basic and also from each other – CUI Specified MUST always be included in the CUI Banner. This is done to ensure that every authorized CUI holder and end-user who receives a document containing CUI Specified knows that the material must be treated in a manner that differs from CUI Basic. This is accomplished in two ways:

1. All CUI Specified documents must include the Category or Subcategory marking for all the CUI Specified contained in that document in the CUI Banner Marking. This ensures that initially, a user in receipt of that document is aware of the CUI Banner. This permits the user to be mindful of whether they have something other than ordinary CUI Basic. It also allows the user to meet any additional or alternative requirements for the CUI Specified they hold.

2. To ensure that it is evident that a Category or Subcategory is Specified, the marking has "SP-" added to the beginning of the marking after the CUI or Controlled designation.

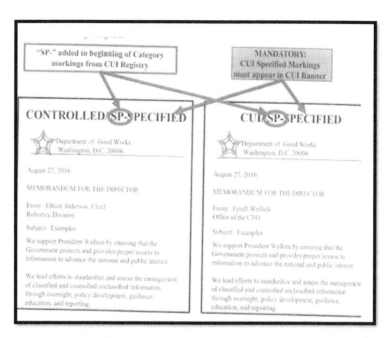

The above examples use the word "SPECIFIED" as a substitute for CUI Category and Subcategory Markings. Consult the CUI Registry for actual CUI markings.

Banner Markings with Multiple of Subcategory Markings (Reference 32 CFR 2002.20)

CUI Specified Markings must precede CUI Basic Markings that were authorized for use by the agency head in the CUI Banner. Consult the agency CUI policy for guidance on the use of CUI Basic Category or Subcategory Markings. Additionally, CUI Category and Subcategory Markings MUST be alphabetized within CUI type (Basic or Specified). Alphabetized Specified CUI categories and subcategories must precede alphabetized Basic CUI categories and subcategories.

Below are examples of CUI Banner Markings used in a document that contains both CUI Specified and CUI Basic.

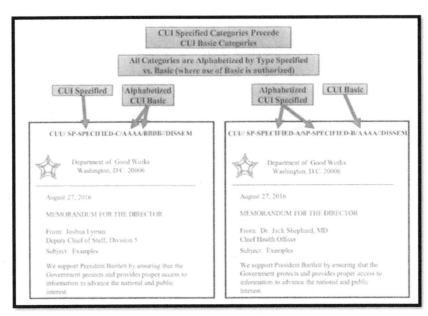

Multiple Category or Subcategory Markings

The above examples use "AAAA" and "BBBB" as substitutes for CUI Basic Category and Subcategory Markings, "SP-SPECIFIED-X" as a substitute for a CUI Specified Category and Subcategory Markings, and "DISSEM" as a substitute for a Limited Dissemination Control Marking. Consult the CUI Registry for actual CUI markings.

Banner Markings (Limited Dissemination Controls)(Reference 32 CFR 2002.20(b)(3)

Only Limited Dissemination (LIMDIS) Control Markings found in the CUI Registry are authorized for use with CUI. Limited Dissemination Control Markings are separated from preceding sections of the CUI Banner Marking by, double forward-slash *(//)*. When a document contains multiple Limited Dissemination Control Markings, those Limited Dissemination Control Markings MUST be alphabetized and separated from each other with a single forward-slash (/).

Below are examples that show the proper use of Limited Dissemination Control Markings in the CUI Banner Marking in a letter-type document or a slide presentation.

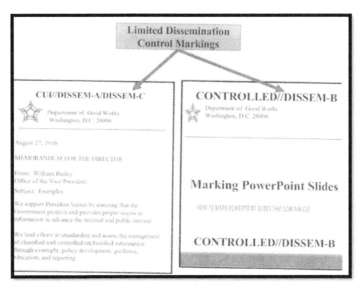

LIMDIS Controls

The above example uses "DISSEM-X" as a substitute for Limited Dissemination Control Markings. Consult the CUI Registry for actual CUI markings.

Designation Indicator (Reference 32 CFR 2002.20(a)(3)(d))

All documents containing CUI must indicate the designator's agency. This may be accomplished with letterhead, a signature block with the agency, or the use of a "Controlled by" line. Every effort should be made to identify a point of contact, branch, or division within an organization responsible for either the creation or protection of the CUI.

Below are examples of Designation Indicators in a slide presentation and a letter-type document.

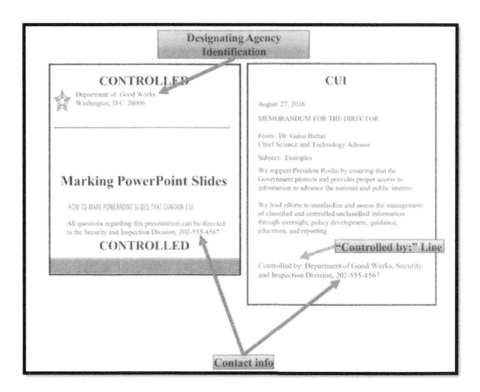

Designation Indicators

Portion Markings (Reference 32 CFR 2002.20(f))

Portion marking of CUI is *optional* in a fully unclassified document but is highly encouraged[9] to facilitate information sharing and proper handling of the information. Agency heads may approve the required use of CUI Portion marking on all CUI generated within their agency. Users should always consult their agency CUI policy when creating CUI documents.

When CUI Portion Marking is used, these rules will be followed. CUI Portion Markings are placed at the beginning of the portion (e.g., beginning of sentence or segment of the CUI), apply it throughout the entire document. CUI Portion Markings are contained within parentheses and may include up to three elements:

---

[9] The author strongly supports the use of portion markings. They further help when providing reports and responding to requests for information from the public; this provides clear boundaries for information release in accordance with the law.

1. The CUI Control Marking: This is mandatory when portion marking and must be the acronym "CUI" (the word "Controlled" will not be used in portion marking).
2. CUI Category or Subcategory Markings: These can be found in the CUI Registry.
    a. When used, CUI Category or Subcategory Markings are separated from the CUI Control Marking by a double forward-slash (//).
    b. When including multiple categories or subcategories in a portion, CUI Category or Subcategory Markings are separated from each other by a single forward-slash (/).
3. Limited Dissemination Control Markings: These can be found in the CUI Registry and are separated from preceding CUI markings by a double forward-slash (//). When including multiple Limited Dissemination Control Markings, they must be alphabetized and separated from each other by a single forward-slash (/).
4. When CUI Portion Markings are used, and a portion does not contain CUI, a "U" is placed in parentheses to indicate that the portion includes Uncontrolled Unclassified Information.

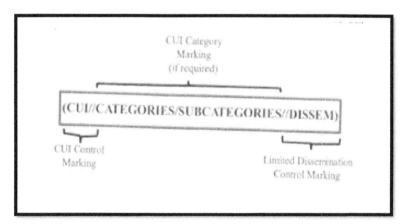

Portion Marking Standards

The above example uses the words "CATEGORIES" and "SUBCATEGORIES" as substitutes for CUI Category or Subcategory Markings and the word "DISSEM" as a substitute for a Limited Dissemination Control Marking. Consult the CUI Registry for actual CUI markings.

The presence of at least one item categorized as CUI in a document requires CUI marking of the entire document. CUI Portion Markings can be of significant assistance in determining if a document contains CUI and, therefore, must be marked appropriately. Additionally, when portion markings are used, and any portion does not include CUI, a "(U)" is placed in front of that portion to indicate that it contains Uncontrolled or non-CUI -Unclassified[10] Information.

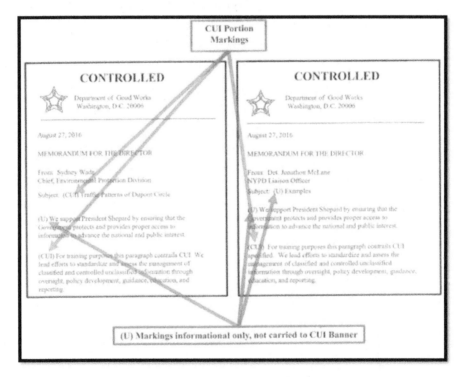

"Parenthetical" Portion Marking Examples

---

[10] Uncontrolled appears to be an ambiguous stamen from NARA; it is best considered as UNCLASSIFIED information that can be freely shared with the general public.

Portion Markings with Category Only (Reference 32 CFR 2002.20(f))

This example shows how to portion mark a document using the CUI Control Marking and CUI Category or Subcategory Markings. When a document contains CUI Specified, all CUI Specified Category or Subcategory Markings must be included in the CUI Banner Marking. Consult your agency CUI policy for guidance on the use of CUI Basic Category or Subcategory Markings. When CUI Portion Markings are used, and a portion does not contain CUI, a "U" is placed in parentheses to indicate that the portion includes Uncontrolled-Unclassified Information.

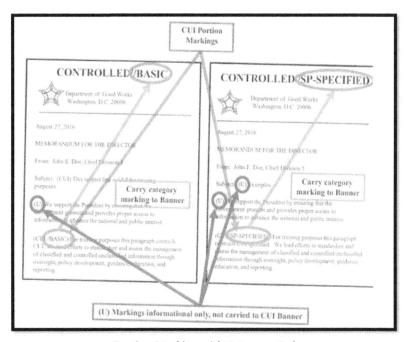

Portion Marking with Category Only

The above example uses "BASIC" and "SPECIFIED" as substitutes for CUI Category or Subcategory Markings. Consult the CUI Registry for actual CUI markings.

Portion Markings with Category and Dissemination Caveats (Reference 32 CFR 2002.20(f))

The example below shows how to portion mark a document using all three components of the CUI Banner Marking. When a document contains CUI Specified, CUI Specified Category or Subcategory Markings must be included in the CUI Banner Marking. Consult your agency CUI policy for guidance on the use of CUI Basic Category or Subcategory Markings. Also, when CUI Portion Markings are used, and a portion does not contain CUI, a "U" is placed in parentheses to indicate that the portion includes Uncontrolled-Unclassified Information.

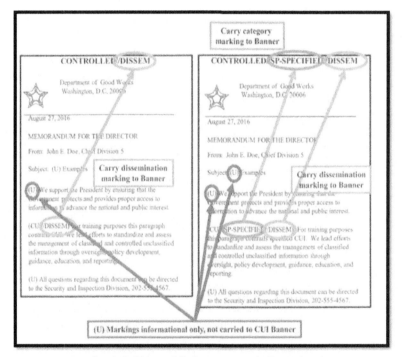

Portion Markings with Category and Dissemination

The above example uses "SP-SPECIFIED" as a substitute for a CUI Category or Subcategory Marking and "DISSEM" as a substitute for Limited Dissemination Control Markings. Consult the CUI Registry for actual CUI markings.

Common Mistakes in Banner Markings

Category and Subcategory Markings for CUI Specified MUST always be included in the Banner Marking, and those for CUI Basic may be required by agency CUI policy. When CUI Portion Markings are used and include CUI Category or Subcategory Markings, those markings MUST be included in the CUI Banner Marking.

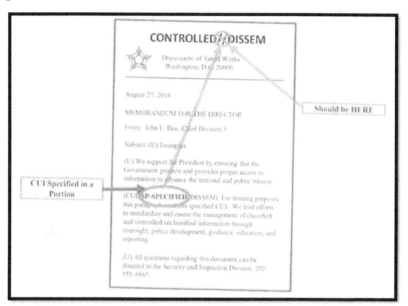

The above example uses "SP-SPECIFIED" as a substitute for a CUI Specified Category or Subcategory Marking and "DISSEM" as a substitute for a Limited Dissemination Control Marking. Consult the CUI Registry for actual CUI markings.

Marking of Multiple Pages (Reference 32 CFR 2002.20(c))

The composition of the CUI Banner Marking for a multi-page document is essentially the totality of all the CUI markings in the document; if any portion of the document contains CUI Specified or a Limited Dissemination Control Marking, then the CUI Banner Marking must reflect that.

Below is an example of one multi-page document with CUI Portion Marking.

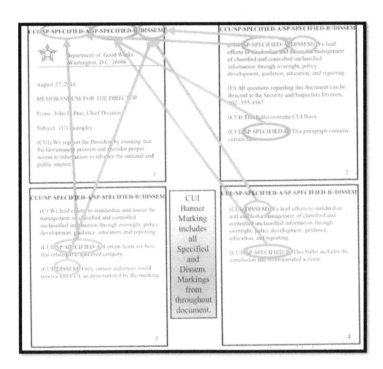

The overall CUI Banner Marking for the document must appear on all pages of the document.

Required Indicators as directed by Authorities (Reference 32 CFR 2002.20 (b)(2)(iii))

Required indicators that include informational, warning, or dissemination statements may be mandated by the law, Federal regulation, or Government-wide policy that makes a specific item of information CUI. These indicators shall not be included in the CUI Banner or portion markings but must appear in a manner readily apparent to authorized personnel. This shall be consistent with the requirements of the governing document.

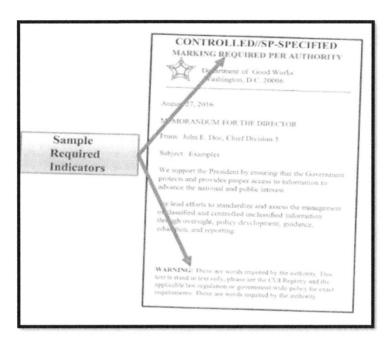

The above example uses "SPECIFIED" as a substitute for a CUI Specified Category or Subcategory Marking. Consult the CUI Registry for actual CUI markings.

Supplemental Administrative Markings (Reference 32 CFR 2002.20(l))

Agencies may use supplemental administrative markings (e.g., Draft, Deliberative, Pre- decisional, Provisional) along with CUI to inform recipients of the non-final status of documents ONLY when such markings are created and defined in agency policy.

Supplemental administrative markings may not be used to control CUI and may not be commingled with or incorporated into the CUI Banner Marking or Portion Markings. Additional administrative markings may not duplicate any marking in the CUI Registry.

Below are two examples of ways to properly use supplemental administrative markings.

Sample Supplemental Administrative Indicators

Common Mistakes for Supplemental Administrative Markings

Supplemental administrative markings may not be used to control CUI and must not be incorporated into CUI Banner Markings or CUI Portion Markings or duplicate any marking in the CUI Registry.

Below are two examples of ways **NOT** to use administrative markings.

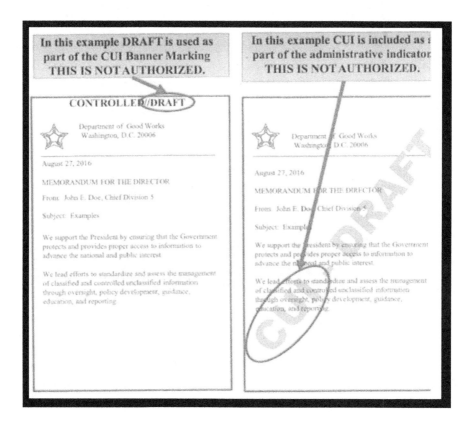

Electronic Media Storage and Marking Procedures (Reference 32 CFR 2002.20)

Media such as USB sticks, hard drives, and CD ROMs must be marked to alert CUI holders to the presence of CUI stored on the device. Due to space limitations, it may not be possible to include Category, Subcategory, or Limited Dissemination Control Markings on the given surface. At a minimum, mark media with the CUI Control Marking ("CONTROLLED" or "CUI") and the Designating Agency. Equipment can be marked or labeled to indicate that CUI is stored on the device.

Removable Hard drive

Equipment can be marked or labeled to indicate that CUI is stored on the device.

NOTE: DOGW is an acronym for Department of Good Works.

Marking Forms (Reference 32 CFR 2002.20)

Forms that contain CUI must be marked when completed. If space on the form is limited, cover sheets can be used for this purpose. As forms are updated during agency implementation of the CUI Program, they should be modified to include a statement that indicates the form is CUI when finalized.

CUI Coversheets (Reference 32 CFR 2002.32)

The use of CUI coversheets is optional except when required by agency policy. Agencies may download coversheets from the CUI Registry or obtain printed copies through the General Services Administration (GSA) Global Supply Centers or the GSAAdvantage online service (https://www.gsa.gov/buying-selling/purchasing-programs/requisition-programs/gsa-global-supply/easy-ordering/gsa-global-supply-online-ordering).

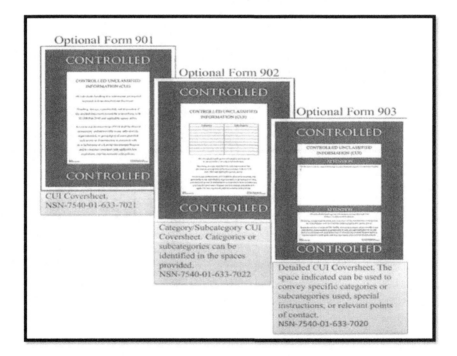

Marking Transmittal Documents (Reference 32 CFR 2002.20)

When a transmittal document accompanies CUI, the transmittal document must indicate that CUI is attached or enclosed. The transmittal document must also include, conspicuously, the following or similar instructions, as appropriate:

- "When the enclosure is removed, this document is Uncontrolled- Unclassified Information"; or
- "When the enclosure is removed, this document is (CUI Control Level); or
- "Upon removal, this document does not contain CUI."

Alternate Marking Methods (Reference 32 CFR 2002.20)

Agency heads[11] may authorize the use of alternate marking methods on IT systems, websites, browsers, or databases through agency CUI policy. These may be used to alert users to the presence of CUI, where the agency head has issued a

---

[11] Agency Heads may be considered federal agency secretaries, leadership, etc., designated under contract to provide direct oversight of the agencies' CUI program.

limited CUI marking waiver for CUI designated within the agency. These warnings may take multiple forms and include the examples below.

Computer Monitor CUI Banners

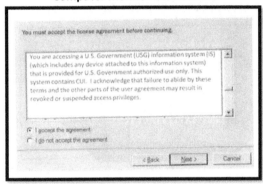

Agency or Company Legal Warning Notification

Room or Area Markings (Reference 32 CFR 2002.20)

In areas containing CUI, it may be necessary to alert personnel who are not authorized to access the area or information. This may be accomplished by any means approved by the agency and detailed in the agency's CUI policy. Typically, signs are posted exterior to the room or rooms, on all entry doors, and in any ante-room designated to verify clearances or need-to-know status of a group or individual.

Below is a sample of a sign that indicates CUI is present.

Example Exterior Door and Interior Rooms Sign

Container Markings (Reference 32 CFR 2002.20)

When an agency is storing CUI, authorized holders should mark the container to indicate that it contains CUI.

Below are some basic examples.

Shipping and Mailing (Reference 32 CFR 2002.20)

Agency heads must ensure that mailroom staffs are trained in handling CUI to include reporting any loss, theft, or misuse.

When shipping CUI:

- Address packages that contain CUI for delivery only to a specific recipient.

- DO NOT put CUI markings on the outside of an envelope or package for mailing/shipping.

- Use in-transit automated tracking and accountability tools where possible.

Re-marking Legacy Information (Reference 32 CFR 2002.36)

Legacy information is unclassified information that was marked as restricted from access or dissemination in some way or otherwise controlled before the CUI Program was established. **All legacy information is not automatically CUI.** Agencies must examine and determine what legacy information qualifies as CUI and mark it accordingly.

In cases of excessive burden, an agency's' head may issue a "Legacy Marking Waiver," as described in 32 CFR 2002.38(b) of the CUI Rule. When the agency head grants such a waiver, legacy material that qualifies need not be re-marked as CUI until and unless it is to be "re-used" in a new document.

"LEGACY MARKING" is used as a substitute for ad hoc, agency markings used to label unclassified information before the creation of the CUI Program.

When legacy information is to be re-used and incorporated into another document of any kind, it must undergo the process described below.

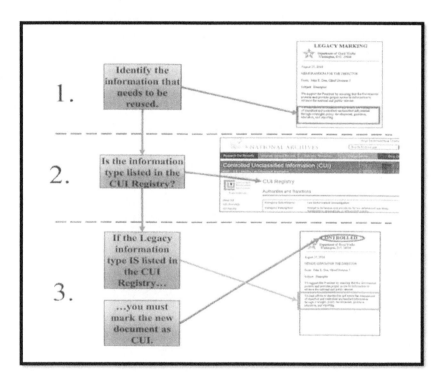

When possible, contact the originator of the information for guidance in remarking and protecting the legacy information in the CUI Program.

CUI MARKINGS IN A CLASSIFIED ENVIRONMENT

Marking Commingled Information (Reference 32 CFR 2002.20(g))

When CUI is included in a document that contains any classified information, that document is referred to as **commingled**. Commingled documents are subject to the requirements of the CUI and Classified National Security Information (CNSI) Programs. As a best practice, keep the CUI and classified information in separate and designated areas to the greatest extent possible[12]. Mark all portions to ensure that authorized holders can distinguish CUI portions from those containing CNSI or Uncontrolled-Unclassified Information; the de-controlling provisions for CUI apply only to portions marked as CUI. CNSI portions remain classified to their declassification requirements.

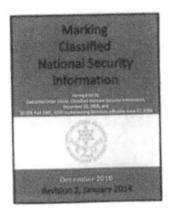

Executive Order 13526 - Classified National Security Information

In the overall marking banner's CUI section, double forward slashes (//) are used to separate significant elements, and single forward slashes (/) are used to separate sub-elements. The CUI Control Marking ("CUI") appears in

---

[12] Typically, classified facilities should be partitioned to include designated drawers, safes, and folders specific to CUI storage.

the overall banner marking directly before the CUI category and subcategory markings. When there is CUI Specified in the document, CUI Specified category and subcategory marking(s) must appear in the overall banner marking. Per agency policy, if used, the optional CUI Basic category and subcategory markings would appear next. Both CUI Specified and CUI Basic markings are separately alphabetized. The limited dissemination control markings apply to the entire document and the CUI and classified information in it. Placeholders are not used for missing elements or sub-elements.

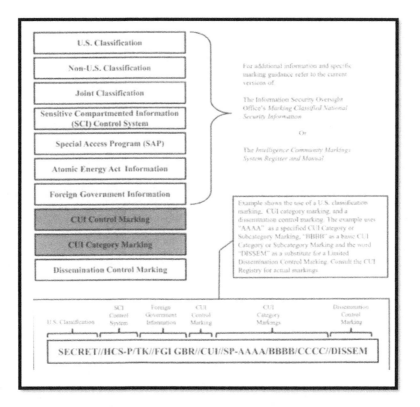

Commingling in the same paragraph is not recommended, where paragraphs contain CUI and CNSI commingled, portion marking elements follow a similar syntax to the banner marking. <u>However, the paragraph always takes the HIGHEST classification of the information contained in the paragraph</u>.

For additional information and specific marking, the guidance refers to the current versions of The Information Security Oversight Office's *Marking Classified National Security Information.*

Commingling Example 1

In cases where CUI is commingled with classified information, the following applies:

- In banners, the CUI Control Marking is used only in its abbreviated form ("CUI"). The longer form ("CONTROLLED") is not used. Either the classification marking, CUI control marking ("CUI"), or the Uncontrolled Unclassified Marking ("U") must be used in every portion.

- Limited Dissemination Control Markings must appear in the banner line and in all portions to which they apply.

Best practice: CUI and CNSI should be placed in separate portions of a document

---

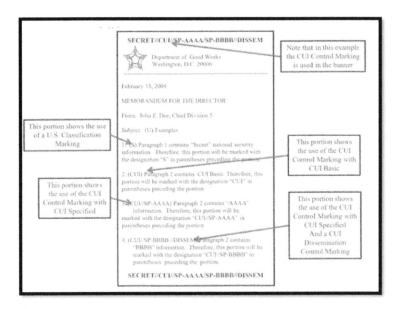

The above examples use "SP-AAAA" or "SP-BBBB" as CUI Specified Category or Subcategory Markings and the word "DISSEM" as a substitute for a Limited Dissemination Control Marking. Consult the CUI Registry for actual markings.

Commingling Example 2

These examples show the various ways CUI may be identified in a document.

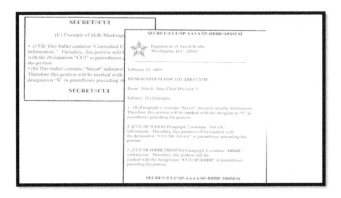

The above examples use "SP-AAAA" or "SP-BBBB" as CUI Specified Category or Subcategory Markings and the word "DISSEM" as a substitute for a Limited Dissemination Control Marking. Consult the CU Registry for actual markings.

Commingling Example 3

Below are two samples of CUI commingled with classified information, specifically with Classified National Security Information (CNSI). The sample on the left has the CUI and CNSI broken into separate paragraphs allowing for more natural future separation when needed to accommodate differing access requirements. The example on the right has CUI and CNSI in the same paragraph.

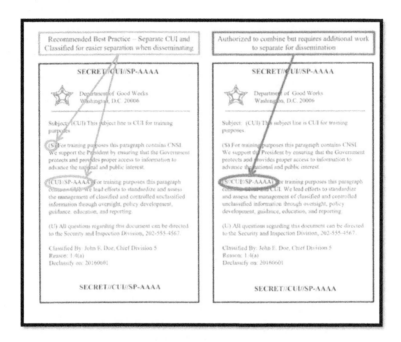

The above examples use the word "SP-AAAA" as a substitute for a CUI Specified Category or Subcategory Marking. Consult the CUI Registry for actual markings.

Commingling Portion Markings (Reference 32 CFR 2002.20(g))

In a commingled document, when a portion contains both CUI and classified information, the portion marking for the classified information must precede the CUI Portion Marking. When commingling CUI with classified information, the user should retain the CUI, and classified portions separate to the greatest extent possible to allow for maximum information sharing. Many of the intricate markings seen below can be avoided by following this simple practice. Below are some examples of how to mark portions containing CUI.

Portion Marking	Contents of Portions Marked Section – CUI ONLY IN PORTION
(CUI)	This section contains CUI Basic.
(CUI//AAAA)	This section contains CUI Basic (with optional category marking).
(CUI//SP-BBBB)	This section contains CUI Specified.
(CUI//SP-BBBB/SP-CCCC)	This section contains two CUI Specified Categories in alphabetical order.
(CUI//DISSEM)	This section contains CUI Basic with a Limited Dissemination Control Marking.
(CUI//AAAA//DISSEM)	This section contains CUI Basic with a Limited Dissemination Control Marking.
(CUI//SP-BBBB/DISSEM)	This section contains CUI Specified with a Limited Dissemination Control Marking.
Portion Marking	**Contents of Portions Marked Section – WITH COMMINGLED PORTIONS (NOT RECOMMENDED)**
(S//CUI)	This section contains Secret information and CUI Basic.
(S//CUI//AAAA)	This section contains Secret information and CUI Basic (with optional category marking).
(S//CUI/SP-BBBB)	This section contains Secret information and CUI Specified.
(S//CUI/SP-BBBB/SP-CCCC)	This section contains Secret information and contains two CUI Specified Categories in alphabetical order.
(S//CUI/SP-BBBB/DISSEM)	This section contains Secret information and CUI Specified with a Limited Dissemination Control Marking.

Using this Book—A "How To"

In June 2018, the NIST issued NIST 800-171A, **"Assessing Security Requirements for Controlled Unclassified Information."** It increased the challenges and complexity of the current federal, *and especially* DOD efforts, to better secure the cybersecurity environment. It added another 298 sub-controls (SUB CTRL), also described within the cybersecurity community as a Control Correlation Identifier (CCI). The *CCI* provides a standard identifier and description for each of the singular, actionable statements that comprise a cybersecurity control or cybersecurity best practice. CCI bridges the gap between high-level policy expressions and low-level technical implementations. CCI allows a security requirement that is expressed in a high-level policy framework to be decomposed and explicitly associated with the low-level security setting(s) that must be assessed to determine compliance with the objectives of that specific security control.

The ability to trace security requirements from their origin (e.g., regulations, cybersecurity frameworks, etc.) to their low-level implementation allows organizations to demonstrate to multiple cybersecurity compliance frameworks readily. CCI also provides a means to objectively rollup and compare related compliance assessment results across disparate technologies.

We are issuing this second edition to better address our work and hope to better assist in this change that will have limited impacts on you and your company or agency. This version will leverage the original version of "Beyond DOD" and provide more details of "how" to answer these additional sub-controls. The effort here will primarily focus on using "examination" mainly to meet the control while suggesting, where appropriate, the use of "testing" and "interviews" are a better approach to answering the sub-controls; most of the recommended strategies will be based upon updates to the company's policy or procedure documents specific to computer security within their respective security boundary.

We have modified the original NIST 800-171A sub-control charts and have added a column to explain suggested approaches to answer the sub-control for a minimal 'compliant' status. We will not attempt to do more than that for this edition.

The generalized assessment from NIST 800-171A only describes an expanded framework and a starting point for developing more specific procedures to assess the CUI security requirements in NIST 800-171 revision 1. ***It does not add new controls; it only provides more detailed enhancements to the base control. There are still 110 controls.*** Edition 1 of this book can still be effectively used to formulate a complete response for contract offices.

Organizations have the flexibility to specialize in their assessment procedures by selecting the specific assessment methods and the set of assessment artifacts to achieve the assessment objectives. There is no expectation that all assessment methods and all artifacts will be used for every assessment. The assessment procedures and methods can be applied using multiple approaches to include self-assessment or independent, third-party assessments. Assessments may also be performed by sponsoring organizations (e.g., government agencies); such procedures may be specified in contracts or agreements by participating parties. Every effort has been attempted in this edition to provide additional information for the sub-control as needed.

Furthermore, assessments can be conducted by systems developers, integrators, assessors, system owners, or their security staff. Assessment teams combine available system information. System assessments can be used to compile and evaluate the evidence needed by organizations and to help determine the effectiveness of the safeguards implemented to protect CUI.

The following key is provided to add brevity where appropriate, and where the previous descriptions in Edition 1 remain complete to answer the sub-control.

ACRONYM	MEANING	DESCRIPTION
NCR	No Change Required	The description and information in the base control are still correct, and there is no further need to modify the original administrative (policy) or technical recommendations.
P	Policy or Procedure	Requires an addition to the company's policy document to answer the sub-control; descriptions or examples are suggested as the "recommended approach" column.
T	A technical solution is needed	Identifies a technical solution is further needed to answer the control or mitigate (reduces) the vulnerability, but not necessarily completely.
PO	Plan of Action & Milestones	The suggestion here is for business owners, where the control appears to be technically challenging to implement, a POAM should be formulated; if able to address, it is always the *preferred* approach to answering any security control.

	W	Waiver or Risk Acceptance	There are some situations—very long-term—where a waiver or risk acceptance, by the company, is a mechanism to accept risk for a control challenging to implement for several years due to lack of expertise, technologically or budget to fulfill the requirement

For this book, the interview method is NOT recommended. While it can be used to verify the quality and completeness of documentation to include, for example, user and administrator manuals, it should not be used on its own. We primarily recommend that document reviews with subsequent technical testing should be the two primary assessment methods. Technical testing of documented processes with associated artifacts is the best approach for a vast majority of the controls cited with NIST 800-171.

Good Processes Provide Good Test Artifact Outputs—
If there are none, then the process has NO value

ACCESS CONTROL (AC)
The most technical, complex, and vital

Access Control (AC) is the most technical and most vital security control family within the cybersecurity process. It is designed to focus computer support personnel, System Administrators (SA), or similar IT staff, on the technical security protections of critical data. This will include any CUI/CDI and internal sensitive data maintained by the company's IT infrastructure and maintained by the company as part of doing business with DOD. If making investments in cybersecurity infrastructure upgrades, the *AC control will provide the highest Return on Investment.*

Also, it is essential to confirm whether either a technical solution is not already embedded in the current IT system. Many times, controls are ignored, captured by policy, or a POAM is developed, even though some base capabilities to address the control are already resident in the base system or, more particularly, within the network Operating System (OS). Also, check for accessory applications provided by the OS manufacturer to determine whether a no-cost solution is already resident. Ask the IT staff to confirm whether there is an existing technical solution as part of the system to avoid spending additional dollars for capabilities already in place.

Where cost is currently prohibitive to implement, a POAM is an acceptable but temporary solution. If unable to address the control during the company's "self-assessment" effort, then be prepared to formulate a Plans of Action and Milestone (POAM). (***Writing an Effective POAM*** is a current supplement to this book on Amazon®).

Sample POAM Template

Basic Security Requirements:

3.1.1 Limit information system access to authorized users, processes acting on behalf of authorized users, or devices (including other information systems). MINIMUM ANSWER: Address this control in the business policy/procedural document. (See example procedure below).

It should identify the types of users and what level of access they are authorized. Typically, some general users have regular daily access to the corporate system data and **elevated/privileged users**.

Elevated/privileged users are usually limited to, for example, System Administrators (SA), Database Administrators (DBA), and other designated Help Desk IT support staff personnel who manage the back-office care of the system; these users usually have **root access**. Root access provides what is more typically described as **super-user** access. These individuals should be highly and regularly screened. These individuals need to be periodically assessed or audited by senior corporate designated personnel.

MORE COMPLETE ANSWER: This should include screen captures that show a sample of employees and their types and kinds of access rights. This could consist of their read, write, edit, delete, etc., **rights** typically controlled by an assigned SA.

We have provided an example of a suggested procedure for this control:

EXAMPLE PROCEDURE: *The company has defined two types of authorized users. There are general users, those that require regular daily access to company automated resources, and privileged users, employees with elevated privileges required to conduct proper back-office care and maintenance of corporate assets and Information Technology (IT) systems. Access to the company's [example] financial, ordering, and human resource systems will be restricted to those general users with a need, based upon their duties, to access these systems. Immediate supervisors will validate their need and advise the IT Help Desk to issue appropriate access credentials [login identification and password] after completing "Cybersecurity Awareness Training." User credentials will not be shared, and…."*

\multicolumn{3}{l}{**ASSESSMENT OBJECTIVE**}
\multicolumn{3}{l}{*Determine if:*}
SUB-CTRL	*DESCRIPTION*	**RECOMMENDED APPROACH**
3.1.1[a]	*Authorized users are identified.*	NCR
3.1.1[b]	*Processes acting on behalf of authorized users are identified.*	P-Processes need to by further defined. This should include access to major applications and their functionality, e.g., finance for finance personnel only, contracting for contract personnel; also, some supervisors will require access to these functional "processes" for oversight purposes.
3.1.1[c]	*Devices (and other systems) authorized to connect to the system are identified.*	SSP-Should identify all devices internal to the security boundary as the primary source document.
3.1.1[d]	*System access is limited to authorized users.*	NCR
3.1.1[e]	*System access is limited to processes acting on behalf of authorized users.*	P-Update policy document that states, "system access is limited to processes acting on behalf of authorized users."
3.1.1[f]	*System access is limited to authorized devices (including other systems).*	P/SSP-State in policy document; should align with SSP.

3.1.2 Limit information system access to the types of transactions and functions that authorized users are permitted to execute.

MINIMUM ANSWER: Address this control in the business policy/procedural document. It should identify the types of transactions and what level is allowed for authorized users. Elevated or privileged users have access to back-office maintenance and care of the network such as account creation, database maintenance, etc.; privileged users can also have general access, but different logins and passwords should segregate their privileges for audit purposes.

MORE COMPLETE ANSWER: This could include a screen capture that shows a sample of employees and their types and kinds of rights. This would consist of their read, write, edit, delete, etc., rights typically controlled by assigned SA. The SA should be able to provide the hardcopy printouts for inclusion into the final submission packet to the DOD contract office or their designated recipient.

ASSESSMENT OBJECTIVE *Determine if:*		
SUB-CTRL	***DESCRIPTION***	**RECOMMENDED APPROACH**
3.1.2[a]	*The types of transactions and functions that authorized users are permitted to execute are defined.*	NCR
3.1.2[b]	*System access is limited to the defined types of transactions and functions for authorized users.*	NCR

Derived (Supplemental) Security Requirements:

3.1.3 Control the flow of CUI flowing the approved authorizations.

MINIMUM ANSWER: Companies typically use **flow control** policies and technologies to manage the movement of CUI/CDI throughout the IT architecture; flow control is based on the types of information.

In terms of procedural updates, discussion of the corporate documents should address several areas of concern: 1) That only authorized personnel within the company with the requisite need-to-know are provided access; 2) appropriate security measures are in place to include encryption while Data is in Transit (DIT); 3) what are the procedures for handling internal employees who violate these company rules?; and, 4) how does the company alert DOD if there is external access (hackers) to its IT infrastructure and its CUI/CDI?

MORE COMPLETE ANSWER: Addressing this control can further be demonstrated by implementing training (See Awareness and Training (AT) control) as a form of **mitigation**; mitigation are other supporting efforts, not just technical, that can reduce the effects of a threat exploits this control. The company could also include risk from insider threats (See Control 3.2.3 for discussion of "insider threat.") by requiring employees to complete Non-disclosure (NDA) and non-compete agreements (NCA). These added measures *reduce or mitigate the risk to the IT infrastructure*. They should also address employees that depart, resign, or are terminated by the company; the consideration is for disgruntled employees that may leave the company with potentially sensitive CUI/CDI.

Flow control could also be better shown to a DOD assessor in terms of a technical solution. This could be further demonstrated by using encryption for DIT and Data at Rest (DAR). These encryption requirements within NIST 800-171 necessitate differing technical solutions, and Federal Information Processing Standards (FIPS) 140-2 compliance; see Control 3.13.11 for more detail.

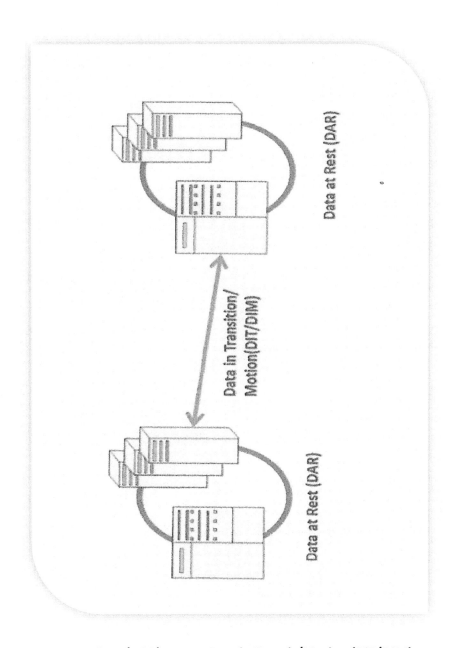

**Data at Rest (DAR) versus Data in Transit/Motion (DIT/DIM)
Conceptual Diagram**

The answer could also include weekly reviews of access logs. Typically, IT support personnel or the SA would conduct recurring audits. If anomalies are detected, what is the procedure to alert senior management to staff attempting access to CUI/CDI and other sensitive data? This offers a more significant demonstration of company security measures to DOD representatives.

ASSESSMENT OBJECTIVE:		
Determine if:		
SUB-CTRL	*DESCRIPTION*	**RECOMMENDED APPROACH**
3.1.3[a]	*Information flow control policies are defined.*	NCR
3.1.3[b]	*Methods and enforcement mechanisms for controlling the flow of CUI are defined.*	NCR (P-especially FIPS 140-2 encryption standards).
3.1.3[c]	*Designated sources and destinations (e.g., networks, individuals, and devices) for CUI within the system and between interconnected systems are identified.*	P/SSP-Add an update to policy/procedure document and a "data flow" diagram to SSP that describes what the flow from the originator to destination involves. At each source or destination, identify whether the data is encrypted or not.
3.1.3[d]	*Authorizations for controlling the flow of CUI are defined.*	NCR
3.1.3[e]	*Approved authorizations for controlling the flow of CUI are enforced.*	P-Updates to the policy should identify the individual or body that can make approved changes to "data flow."

3.1.4 Separate the duties of individuals to reduce the risk of malevolent activity without collusion.

MINIMUM ANSWER: This should be described in the corporate cybersecurity procedural document and should identify the roles and responsibilities of how oversight will be executed. When this is difficult, based on the size and limited IT personnel, a POAM is highly recommended.

The POAM should suggest other ways used to mitigate such a **risk**, and potentially look at both human and automated means to better address in the future.

MORE COMPLETE ANSWER: Individuals should be assigned *in-writing* and their roles and responsibilities. This could also include the reporting thresholds of unauthorized activities and who is alerted internal threats; this would better provide a more defined solution. It also could address Human Resource (HR) challenges when such incidents occur and provide a means of action against violators of corporate policy.

ASSESSMENT OBJECTIVE *Determine if:*		
SUB-CTRL	**DESCRIPTION**	**RECOMMENDED APPROACH**
3.1.4[a]	The duties of individuals requiring separation are defined.	NCR
3.1.4[b]	Responsibilities for duties that require separation are assigned to separate individuals.	NCR
3.1.4[c]	Access privileges that enable individuals to exercise the duties that require separation are granted to separate individuals.	NCR

3.1.5 Employ the principle of least privilege, including for specific security functions and privileged accounts.

MINIMUM ANSWER: The principle of least privilege is a vital cybersecurity tenet. The concept of least privilege is about allowing only authorized access for users and processes that they have direct responsibility. It is limited to only a necessary level of access to accomplish tasks for specific business functions. This should be described in the corporate cybersecurity policy document. This should also be part of basic user agreements to include what is described in DOD terminology, an **Acceptable Use Policy** (AUP).

MORE COMPLETE ANSWER: Much like the controls described above, a sampling of employees' print-outs or screen captures could show selected and authorized individual rights. A sampling, especially of privileged users and their assigned roles within the company's IT infrastructure, would be a target of potential third-party DOD assessors. This would be used by assessors to support the developing NIST 800-171 certification process.

ASSESSMENT OBJECTIVE *Determine if:*		
SUB-CTRL	*DESCRIPTION*	**RECOMMENDED APPROACH**
3.1.5[a]	*Privileged accounts are identified.*	P-Should have a list of privileged users as an ongoing artifact.
3.1.5[b]	*Access to privileged accounts is authorized in accordance with the principle of least privilege.*	NCR
3.1.5[c]	*Security functions are identified.*	NCR
3.1.5[d]	*Access to security functions is authorized in accordance with the principle of least privilege.*	NCR

3.1.6 Use non-privileged accounts or roles when accessing nonsecurity functions.

MINIMUM ANSWER: It is best to always first answer controls from a policy or procedural solution. Essentially, this is preventing "general users" from accessing the corporate infrastructure and creating accounts, deleting databases, or elevating their privileges to gain access to both CUI/CDI and sensitive corporate data. This is about providing the least amount of access and privilege based upon the duties assigned. Companies will see the control below that mandates a separation not just of duties, but access as well based on position and a clear need-to-know.

MORE COMPLETE ANSWER: The more-complete answer could be through automated solutions that monitor access to other security functions such as password resets, account creation, etc. This could include logging and review of all system access. It could also include automated tools that restrict access based upon a user's rights. These technical settings within the tool are established by company policy and monitored by, for example, the local SA.

ASSESSMENT OBJECTIVE *Determine if:*		
SUB-CTRL	***DESCRIPTION***	**RECOMMENDED APPROACH**
3.1.6[a]	*Nonsecurity functions are identified.*	NCR
3.1.6[b]	*Users are required to use non-privileged accounts or roles when accessing nonsecurity functions.*	P-This statement should be part of the company policy: "Users are required to use non-privileged accounts or roles when accessing nonsecurity functions." (Best way to ensure completeness).

3.1.7 Prevent non-privileged users from executing privileged functions and audit the execution of such functions.

MINIMUM ANSWER: There are many apparent similarities of the controls, and that was initially designed into NIST 800-171 for a reason. Security controls are supposed to be reinforcing, and this control is only slightly different in its scope than others described earlier.

Control 3.1.6 is similar is reinforcing this control as well as others. The company's procedure guide can explicitly "rewrite" the original control description: "Prevent non-privileged users from executing privileged functions...." An example procedure write-up based upon the original control description is provided:

EXAMPLE PROCEDURE: *Non-privileged users are prohibited from executing any privileged functions or system audits without the authority of the company's Chief Operating Officer, Chief Information Security Officer, or their designated representative. All requests will be submitted in writing with their first-line supervisor, validating the need for such access for a limited and specified time.*

Additionally, this procedure limits higher-order (privileged) functions such as creating accounts for others, deleting database files, etc. It also requires the auditing of all privileged services. It is suggested that the assigned SA at least weekly review and report inconsistencies of non-privileged/general users attempting (and, hopefully failing) to access parts of the internal infrastructure.

MORE COMPLETE ANSWER: A more thorough representation would be to provide copies of audit logs that include who, when, and what were the results of an audit evaluation; these artifacts should demonstrate that the company is following its internal cybersecurity procedures.

NOTE ABOUT "FREQUENCY": Many of the controls do not define how often a business should conduct a review, reassessment, etc. The business owner is allowed to "define success" to the DOD Contract Officer or cybersecurity assessor. The critical consideration is that the business determines the frequency of reviews, in general, based upon the perceived or actual sensitivity of the data. This book will typically provide the more stringent DOD frequency standard, but nothing prevents a company from conducting less often reviews if it can be substantiated.

ASSESSMENT OBJECTIVE *Determine if:*		
SUB-CTRL	*DESCRIPTION*	**RECOMMENDED APPROACH**
3.1.7[a]	*Privileged functions are defined.*	NCR
3.1.7[b]	*Non-privileged users are defined.*	NCR
3.1.7[c]	*Non-privileged users are prevented from executing privileged functions.*	NCR
3.1.7[d]	*The execution of privileged functions is captured in audit logs.*	P- Example policy statement update might read as: "*privileged functions are always captured and reviewed within audit logs weekly.*"

 "Define your own success."

3.1.8 Limit unsuccessful logon attempts.

MINIMUM ANSWER: DOD standard policy is after three failed logins; the system will automatically lock out the individual. Suggest this should be no more than five failed logins, especially if employees are not computer savvy. This requires both the technical solution by the corporate IT system and described in the corporate procedure guide.

MORE COMPLETE ANSWER: For example, the additional ability to provide a screen capture that provides an artifact showing what happens when an employee reaches the maximum number of logons would meet this control; this could be added to the submission packet. It is also essential to document procedures to include the process to regain network access.

ASSESSMENT OBJECTIVE *Determine if:*		
SUB-CTRL	*DESCRIPTION*	**RECOMMENDED APPROACH**
3.1.8[a]	*The means of limiting unsuccessful logon attempts is defined.*	T-This is looking for what is monitoring unsuccessful logons. It could be as necessary as: "The XYZ Operating System enforces failed logon attempts after 3 fails."
3.1.8[b]	*The defined means of limiting unsuccessful logon attempts is implemented.*	T-(See above)

3.1.9 Provide privacy and security notices consistent with applicable CUI rules. MINIMUM ANSWER: Provided below is a current version of the **DOD Warning Banner** designed for company purposes. It should either be physically posted on or near each terminal or on the on-screen logon (preferred); this should also always include consent to monitoring. Recommend consulting with a legal representative for final approval and dissemination to employees.

[Company] Warning Banner

Use of this or any other [Company name] computer system constitutes consent to monitoring at all times.

This is a [Company name] computer system. All [Company name] computer systems and related equipment are intended for the communication, transmission, processing, and storage of official or other authorized information only. All [Company name] computer systems are subject to monitoring at all times to ensure the proper functioning of equipment and systems, including security devices and systems, to

prevent unauthorized use and violations of statutes and security regulations, to deter criminal activity, and for other similar purposes. Any user of a [Company name] computer system should be aware that any information placed in the system is subject to monitoring and is not subject to any expectation of privacy.

If monitoring of this or any other [Company name] computer system reveals possible evidence of the violation of criminal statutes, this evidence, and any other related information, including identification information about the user, may be provided to law enforcement officials. If monitoring of this or any other [Company name] computer systems reveals violations of security regulations or unauthorized use, employees who violate security regulations or make unauthorized use of [Company name] computer systems are subject to appropriate disciplinary action.

Use of this or any other [Company name] computer system constitutes consent to monitoring at all times.

MORE COMPLETE ANSWER: Another consideration should be that this policy also is coordinated with Human Resources (HR). This could further include that all employees sign a copy of this notice, and it is placed in their official file. Select and redacted copies could be used to demonstrate an active adherence to this requirement as a sampling provided to DOD. It could also potentially describe how the company can act against personnel who fail or violate this warning.

ASSESSMENT OBJECTIVE *Determine if:*		
SUB-CTRL	*DESCRIPTION*	**RECOMMENDED APPROACH**
3.1.9[a]	*Privacy and security notices required by CUI-specified rules are identified, consistent, and associated with the specific CUI category.*	NCR
3.1.9[b]	*Privacy and security notices are displayed.*	NCR (This can be either physically displayed or when

			logging in [preferred]).

3.1.10. Use session lock with pattern-hiding displays to prevent access/viewing of data after a period of inactivity.

MINIMUM ANSWER: While this may appear as solely a technical solution, it too should be identified in the company policy or procedure document. Session lock describes the period of inactivity when a computer terminal will automatically lock out the user. Suggest no more than 10 minutes for a computer lockout. Selecting longer is acceptable based upon many factors such as the type of work done (e.g., finance personnel) or the physical security level of the business (e.g., a restricted area with a limited number of authorized employees) is acceptable. However, be prepared to defend the balance between the company's need to meet DOD mission requirements and the risks of excessive session lock timeouts.

Secondarily, **Pattern Hiding** is desired to prevent the concept of "shoulder surfing." Other like terms that are synonymous include **masking** and **obfuscation**.

> Password without Pattern Hiding: PA$$w0rD
>
> Password with Pattern Hiding:

Pattern hiding is designed to prevent an individual from observing an employee typing their password or Personal Identification Number (PIN). This control could include asterisks (*), for example, that mask the true information. This prevents insiders or even visitors from "stealing" another user's login credentials.

MORE COMPLETE ANSWER: The better solution could include much shorter periods for a time-out, and longer password length and complexity; the DOD standard is at least 15 alpha-numeric and special characters.

- Alpha: abcde….
- Numeric: 12345…
- Special Characters: @ # $ % ….

(See Control 3.13.10 for a further discussion of **Multifactor Authentication (MFA)** and **Two Factor Authentication (2FA)).**

As an ongoing reminder, it is critical to place artifacts describing the technical solution demonstrated, for example, using screen capture. It should be clear and easily traceable to this control's implementation by a DOD audit representative or assessor.

ASSESSMENT OBJECTIVE *Determine if:*		
SUB-CTRL	*DESCRIPTION*	**RECOMMENDED APPROACH**
3.1.10[a]	*The period of inactivity after which the system initiates a session lock is defined.*	NCR
3.1.10[b]	*Access to the system and viewing of data is prevented by initiating a session lock after the defined period of inactivity.*	NCR
3.1.10[c]	*Previously visible information is concealed via a pattern-hiding display after the defined period of inactivity.*	NCR

3.1.11. Terminate (automatically) a user session after a defined condition.
MINIMUM ANSWER: The simplest solution is a setting that the SA or other designated IT personnel, sets within the network's operating and management applications. Typically, most network operating systems can be set to enforce a terminal/complete lockout. This control implementation completely logs out the user and terminates any communications' sessions to include, for example, access to corporate databases, financial systems, or the Internet. It requires employees to re-initiate session connections to the network after this more-complete session logout occurs.

MORE COMPLETE ANSWER: The complete answer could include screen captures of policy settings for session terminations and time-outs. The SA or designated company representative should be able to provide as an artifact.

ASSESSMENT OBJECTIVE Determine if:		
SUB-CTRL	DESCRIPTION	RECOMMENDED APPROACH
3.1.11[a]	Conditions requiring a user session to terminate are defined.	NCR
3.1.11[b]	A user session is automatically terminated after any of the defined conditions occur.	NCR

3.1.12 Monitor and control remote access sessions.

MINIMUM ANSWER: This control is about remote access where one computer can control another computer over the Internet. This may include desktop support personnel "remoting into" an employee's computer to update the latest version of Firefox ® or a work-at-home employee inputting financial data into the corporate finance system. Identify these types of access as part of the procedural guide and describe who is authorized, how their access is limited (such as a finance employee cannot issue themselves a corporate check), and the repercussions of violating the policy.

MORE COMPLETE ANSWER: The better technological approach could include restrictions to only IT help personnel using remote capabilities. Company policy should require regular review of auditable events and logs. A screen capture would be helpful to show the policy settings specific to the remote desktop application.

ASSESSMENT OBJECTIVE Determine if:		
SUB-CTRL	DESCRIPTION	RECOMMENDED APPROACH
3.1.12[a]	Remote access sessions are permitted.	P-Only for authorized personnel with a clear need
3.1.12[b]	The types of permitted remote access are identified.	NCR
3.1.12[c]	Remote access sessions are controlled.	NCR

3.1.12[d]	*Remote access sessions are monitored.*	P-Recommend that these sessions be logged for all users.

3.1.13 Employ cryptographic mechanisms to protect the confidentiality of remote access sessions.

MINIMUM ANSWER: *This is a Data in Transit (DIT) issue*. Ensure the procedure requires the company's solution only uses approved cryptographic solutions. The **Advanced Encryption Standard** (AES) is considered the current standard for encryption within DOD and the federal government. Also, use the 256 kilobytes (kb) key length versions.

There are many commercial solutions in this area. Major software companies provide solutions that secure DIT and are typically at reasonable prices for small business options such as Symantec ®, McAfee ®, and Microsoft®.

 Again, document, document, document

MORE COMPLETE ANSWER: (See Control 3.1.3 for a more detailed representation). It is usually a capability directly afforded by the remote access application tool providers. The more critical issue within DOD is whether the application tool company ensures the application is coming from a US-based software developer.

There are many overseas developers, for example, to include Russia, former Warsaw Pact countries, and China, that are of concern to DOD. The apprehension is about commercial products from these nations and their potential threat to US national security. The business should confirm that the product is coming from a current ally of the US; these would include the United Kingdom, Australia, etc. *Before purchasing, ensure you have done your homework, and provide proof the remote access software is accepted by DOD.*

ASSESSMENT OBJECTIVE *Determine if:*		
SUB-CTRL	*DESCRIPTION*	**RECOMMENDED APPROACH**
3.1.13[a]	Cryptographic mechanisms to protect the confidentiality of remote access sessions are identified.	NCR
3.1.13[b]	Cryptographic mechanisms to protect the confidentiality of remote access sessions are implemented.	NCR

3.1.14 Route remote access via managed access control points.

MINIMUM ANSWER: **Managed access control** points are about control of traffic through "trusted" connections. For example, this could be Verizon ® or AT&T® as the company's Internet Service Provider (ISP). It would be highly recommended to include any contracted services or Service Level Agreements (SLA)[13] from these providers. They may consist of additional threat and spam filtering services that could reduce the "bad guys" from gaining access to corporate data; these are ideal artifacts for proof of satisfactorily meeting this control.

MORE COMPLETE ANSWER: Another addition could also be using what is called a **Virtual Private Network (VPN).** These are also common services the significant providers have for additional costs.

Describing and providing such agreements to DOD could also identify a **defense in depth** approach; the first level is through the VPN service, and the second would be provided by the remote access software providing an additional layer of defense. Defense in depth can include such protective efforts to prevent unauthorized access to company IT assets:

- Physical protection (e.g., alarms, guards)

---

[13] See the latest version of "**The Cloud Service Level Agreement (CSLA): A Supplement for NIST 800-171 Implementation**" on Amazon for more information about the CSLA when seeking to deploy part or all of the corporate IT environment with a Cloud Service Provider (CSP).

- Perimeter (e.g., firewalls, Intrusion Detection System (IDS), "Trusted Internet Connections")
- Application/Executables (e.g., **whitelisting** of authorized software, **blacklisting** blocking specified programs)
- Data (e.g., Data Loss Protection programs, Access controls, auditing)

ASSESSMENT OBJECTIVE *Determine if:*		
SUB-CTRL	DESCRIPTION	RECOMMENDED APPROACH
3.1.14[a]	Managed access control points are identified and implemented.	NCR
3.1.14[b]	Remote access is routed through managed network access control points.	NCR

3.1.15 Authorize remote execution of privileged commands and remote access to security-relevant information.

MINIMUM ANSWER: NIST 800-53 is the base document for all controls of NIST 800-171. It describes what businesses should manage and authorize privileged access to **security-relevant** information (e.g., finance information, IP, etc.), and using remote access only for "compelling operational needs."

This would explicitly be documented in the restrictions of who and under what circumstances security-relevant information may be accessed by company personnel. The base NIST control requires the business documents the rationale for this access in the System Security Plan (SSP); the interpretation is that the corporate cybersecurity policy should be an annex or appendix to the **SSP**. (See *"System Security Plan (SSP) Template and Workbook"* on Amazon®)

MORE COMPLETE ANSWER: The ideal artifact suggested are the logs of remote access within and external to the company. This could also be found in the firewall audit logs as well as the remote access software application logs for comparison; these could also be used to identify log modifications that may be an indicator of **insider threat**. (See Control 3.2.3 for further discussion of this topic area).

ASSESSMENT OBJECTIVE *Determine if:*		
SUB-CTRL	*DESCRIPTION*	**RECOMMENDED APPROACH**
3.1.15[a]	*Privileged commands authorized for remote execution are identified.*	P-Updates to policy should identify those "commands" that could compromise data such as changing prices, for example, without a requisite second party review, i.e., "separation of duty."
3.1.15[b]	*Security-relevant information authorized to be accessed remotely is identified.*	NCR
3.1.15[c]	*The execution of the identified privileged commands via remote access is authorized.*	NCR
3.1.15[d]	*Access to the identified security-relevant information via remote access is authorized.*	NCR

3.1.16 Authorize wireless access prior to allowing such connections.
MINIMUM ANSWER: This would include wireless access agreements and, more commonly described earlier, is an Acceptable Use Policy (AUP). For example, an AUP would consist of defining the types and kinds of sites restricted from access by employees. These are typically gambling, pornography sites, etc. A lawyer should review AUP's before requiring employees to sign.

MORE COMPLETE ANSWER: The more-complete technical solution could identify unapproved sites and prevent "guest" access. (While guest access is not recommended, it is better to establish a secondary Wi-Fi network to accommodate and restrict visitors and third-party personnel from having direct access to the company network.)

It is also essential that the Wi-Fi network topology and encryption standard be provided as an artifact to DOD once the final packet is ready for submission. This should be part of the SSP and the corporate cybersecurity procedure document.

ASSESSMENT OBJECTIVE Determine if:		
SUB-CTRL	DESCRIPTION	RECOMMENDED APPROACH
3.1.16[a]	Wireless access points are identified.	NCR (Specifically, part of the SSP)
3.1.16[b]	Wireless access is authorized prior to allowing such connections.	NCR

3.1.17 Protect wireless access using authentication and encryption.

MINIMUM ANSWER: Ensure this is included in the corporate procedure or policy that only authorized personnel within the firm to have access and that the appropriate level of encryption is in place. Currently, the 802.11 standard is used, and Wi-Fi Protected Access 2 (WPA2) encryption should be the minimum standard.

MORE COMPLETE ANSWER: Use of Wi-Fi "sniffing technology" while available may be prohibitively costly to smaller businesses. This technology can identify and audit unauthorized entry into the wireless portion of the network and subsequently provides access to the "physical" company network. Sniffers can be used to notify security personnel either through email or Short Message Service (SMS)-text alerts of such intrusions; if company data is highly sensitive, then this investment may be necessary. Also, maintain any documentation about the "sniffer" and its capabilities; provide it to DOD representatives as part of the official submission.

ASSESSMENT OBJECTIVE Determine if:		
SUB-CTRL	DESCRIPTION	RECOMMENDED APPROACH
3.1.17[a]	Wireless access to the system is protected using authentication.	NCR

| 3.1.17[b] | Wireless access to the system is protected using encryption. | NCR |

3.1.18. Control connection of mobile devices.

MINIMUM ANSWER: Most businesses' mobile devices are their cell phones. This would also include laptops and computer "pads" with web-enabled capabilities. This would first require as a matter of policy that employees only use secure connections for their devices when not using the company's service provider—these should be verified as secure. This would also explicitly bar employee's use of unsecured Wi-fi **hot spots** such as fast-food restaurants, coffee shops, etc. Home Wi-fi networks are typically secure but ensure that employees know to select **WPA2** as their standard at-home secure connection protocol.

MORE COMPLETE ANSWER: A better way to demonstrate this control is by discussing with the cell phone provider the ability to prevent corporate phones from using insecure Wi-Fi networks at any time. The provider should be able to block access if the mobile phone does not "see" or recognize a secure connection. Include any proof from service agreements of such a provision as part of the submitted BOE.

ASSESSMENT OBJECTIVE *Determine if:*		
SUB-CTRL	*DESCRIPTION*	**RECOMMENDED APPROACH**
3.1.18[a]	*Mobile devices that process, store, or transmit CUI are identified.*	P-Ensure an artifact is updated with carriers at least monthly (recommended)
3.1.18[b]	*Mobile device connections are authorized.*	NCR
3.1.18[c]	*Mobile device connections are monitored and logged.*	P/T-Policy and notification to users should be documented and signed by every user (e.g., the AUP), and the carrier provides logs

			as requested or required.

3.1.19. Encrypt CUI on mobile devices.

MINIMUM ANSWER: The good news is that all the major carriers provide DAR encryption. Mobile phones typically can secure DAR on the phone behind a passcode, PIN, or even biometric capability such as fingerprint or facial recognition; these are acceptable by DOD standards. Check service agreements or add to the company's existing plan.

MORE COMPLETE ANSWER: Several companies provide proprietary and hardened devices for corporate users. These include state of the art encryption standards and further hardened phone bodies to prevent physical exploits of lost or stolen mobile devices. *Expect these solutions to be costly.*

ASSESSMENT OBJECTIVE *Determine if:*		
SUB-CTRL	***DESCRIPTION***	***RECOMMENDED APPROACH***
3.1.19[a]	*Mobile devices and mobile computing platforms that process, store, or transmit CUI are identified.*	NCR
3.1.19[b]	*Encryption is employed to protect CUI on identified mobile devices and mobile computing platforms.*	NCR

3.1.20 Verify and control/limit connections to and use of external systems.

MINIMUM ANSWER: This control requires that all external or third-party connections to the company's network be verified. This would typically take the form of accepting another company (or even DOD agencies') Authority to Operate (ATO). This could be as simple as a memorandum, for example, recognizing another company's self-assessment under NIST 800-171. It could also be accepted through a process known as **reciprocity**, of accepting an ATO based upon NIST 800-53—more typical of DOD and other federal agencies. These are all legitimate means that are designed to ensure before a company allows another company to enter through its firewall (system security boundary) without some level of certainty that security was thoroughly considered. Before an external system or network is allowed unfettered access to the corporations' data, it is critical to identify the rules and restrictions for such access as part of this control.

As always, ensure procedures identify and limit, such connections to only critical data feeds needed from third-parties to conduct formal business operations.

MORE COMPLETE ANSWER: This could include a request for ongoing scans of the external system or network every 30 days; this would be considered quite extreme, but dependent on data sensitivity. If sought, suggest that every six-month that the company receives copies of the anti-virus, anti-malware, and vulnerability patch scanning reports identifying current threats to the external system. This is designed to address inbound threats potentially and to enhance the company's overall security posture.

ASSESSMENT OBJECTIVE *Determine if:*		
SUB-CTRL	*DESCRIPTION*	RECOMMENDED APPROACH
3.1.20[a]	*Connections to external systems are identified.*	SSP-Should be identified in the architecture diagram
3.1.20[b]	*The use of external systems is identified.*	SSP-(See above)
3.1.20[c]	*Connections to external systems are verified.*	NCR
3.1.20[d]	*The use of external systems is verified.*	NCR
3.1.20[e]	*Connections to external systems are controlled/limited.*	NCR
3.1.20[f]	*The use of external systems is controlled/limited.*	NCR

3.1.21 Limit use of organizational portable storage devices on external systems.
MINIMUM ANSWER: This is not only about the use of USB thumb drives (see Chapter on Media Protection (MP)), it is also about external drives attached to a workstation or

laptop, locally. While thumb drives are more capable of introducing malware and viruses to an unprotected network, external drives pose a real threat to data removal and theft. The company policy should include an approval process to "attach" only company provided drives and highly discourage personal devices attached by employees. Technical support should consist of the active scanning for viruses and malware every time the portable device is connected to the network.

MORE COMPLETE ANSWER: As discussed in more detail below regarding the use of thumb drives, IT personnel could disable anyone from using the **registry**. Where the need for external drives is necessitated, this control can be further enhanced through auditing of all such attachments and provide pre-formatted reports for company leadership. Auditing, as described under the AU control, should include capturing this activity.

ASSESSMENT OBJECTIVE *Determine if:*		
SUB-CTRL	*DESCRIPTION*	**RECOMMENDED APPROACH**
3.1.21[a]	*The use of portable storage devices containing CUI on external systems is identified and documented.*	NCR
3.1.21[b]	*Limits on the use of portable storage devices containing CUI on external systems are defined.*	NCR
3.1.21[c]	*The use of portable storage devices containing CUI on external systems is limited as defined.*	NCR

3.1.22 Control CUI posted or processed on publicly accessible systems.
MINIMUM ANSWER: This addresses the control of publicly accessible information most commonly on the company's **public-facing** website. There needs to be procedural guidance and direction about who can release (usually public affairs office, etc.) and post information (usually webmaster, etc.) to the website. This should include a review of such data by personnel specifically trained to recognize CUI/CDI data. This may

include information or data that discusses a company's current business relationship with the DOD, the activities it conducts, and the products and services it provides to both the public and private sectors.

This should also address the regular review of publicly accessible data, and the procedure to describe the process to remove unauthorized data if discovered.

MORE COMPLETE ANSWER: This could use automated scans of keywords and phrases that may alert audit personnel during their regular auditing activities. See the Auditing Control (AU) chapter. While this is a static means to alert untrained IT personnel, it could supplement that inadvertent release does not occur. Additional oversight should always be based upon the sensitivity of the information handled to not only include CUI/CDI but Intellectual Property (IP) or other sensitive data, etc., that may harm the company if released into the public.

ASSESSMENT OBJECTIVE *Determine if:*		
SUB-CTRL	*DESCRIPTION*	**RECOMMENDED APPROACH**
3.1.22[a]	*Individuals authorized to post or process information on publicly accessible systems are identified.*	NCR
3.1.22[b]	*Procedures to ensure CUI is not posted or processed on publicly accessible systems are identified.*	NCR
3.1.22[c]	*A review process is in place prior to posting of any content to publicly accessible systems.*	NCR
3.1.22[d]	*Content on publicly accessible systems is reviewed to ensure that it does not include CUI.*	NCR
3.1.22[e]	*Mechanisms are in place to remove and address improper posting of CUI.*	NCR

🔒 *The decision process of how much encryption and added protection (such as hashing or emerging blockchain encryption technologies) should be based on the risk to the IT system.*

☠️ *Consider the risk and the damage to the company if the data, CUI or not, is compromised*

AWARENESS & TRAINING (AT)
A training program is a must

    Awareness & Training is about an active cybersecurity training program for employees and a recurring education program that ensures their familiarity and compliance with protecting sensitive and CUI/CDI company data consistently. The websites (below) identify FREE government-sponsored sites a company can leverage without expending any of its resources. The three major training requirements that can be expected of most vendors supporting federal government contract activities include:

1. **Cybersecurity Awareness Training.**
   https://securityawareness.usalearning.gov/cybersecurity/index.htm

2. **Insider Threat Training.**
   https://securityawareness.usalearning.gov/itawareness/index.htm
   (More discussion on the "Insider Threat" topic See Control 3.2.3).

3. **Privacy.** https://iatraining.disa.mil/eta/piiv2/launchPage.htm (This would correctly apply to any company that handles, processes, or maintains Personally Identifiable Information (PII) and Personal Health Information (PHI). The author expects that even though a company does not handle PII or PHI, the federal government will direct this as a universal training requirement.)

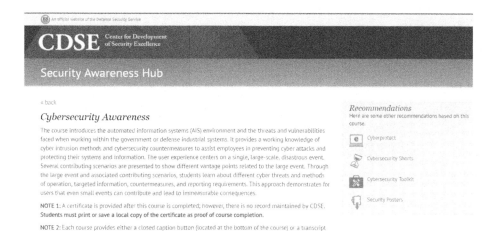

Defense Security Service (DSS) Cybersecurity Awareness Site

Basic Security Requirements:

3.2.1 Ensure that managers, systems administrators, and users of organizational information systems are made aware of the security risks associated with their activities and of the applicable policies, standards, and procedures related to the security of organizational information systems.

MINIMUM ANSWER: Human beings are the weakest link in the cybersecurity "war." The greatest threat is from the employee who unwittingly selects a link that allows an intrusion into the corporate system, or worse, those who maliciously remove, modify or delete sensitive CUI/CDI.

The answer should be documented regarding initial and annual refresher training requirements for everyone in the company, not average employees but must include senior managers and support subcontractors. Provide a sampling of select employees that have taken the training and ensuring it is current within the past year.

MORE COMPLETE ANSWER: A possible demonstration of the more-complete solution is within the policy specific direction to IT support personnel. There could be a system notification that allows them after notification, manually or by automated means, to suspend access to training is completed. Substantial documentation is important specific to awareness training.

ASSESSMENT OBJECTIVE		
Determine if:		
SUB-CTRL	*DESCRIPTION*	**RECOMMENDED APPROACH**
3.2.1[a]	*Security risks associated with organizational activities involving CUI are identified.*	P-This would take the form of an initial and follow-on Risk Assessment (RA) for this control. Recommend an RA is conducted by the CIO, CISO, or like IT representative who conducts and review this review with senior leadership annually.
3.2.1[b]	*Policies, standards, and procedures related to the security of the system are identified.*	P- "*Policies, standards, and procedures related to the security of the system are identified AND DOCUMENTED annually in conjunction with a company RA [see above].*"
3.2.1[c]	*Managers, systems administrators, and users of the system are made aware of the security risks associated with their activities.*	P-Add to current and future updates to cybersecurity awareness training specific to an RA.
3.2.1[d]	*Managers, systems administrators, and users of the system are made aware of the applicable policies, standards, and procedures related to the security of the system.*	P-Add to current and future updates to cybersecurity awareness training specific to an RA.

3.2.2 Ensure that organizational personnel are adequately trained to carry out their assigned information, security-related duties and responsibilities.
MINIMUM ANSWER: This is required not only awareness training but also specialized training for privileged users. This is usually an Operating System (OS) training specific to

the company's architecture. It is possible to have multiple OS's. Privileged users are only required to show, for example, some form of the training certificate, to meet this requirement. All IT personnel who have elevated privileges must have such training before they are authorized to execute their duties.

Additionally, if the company uses Microsoft ® or Linux ® Operating Systems, privileged users will have some level of certification to show familiarity with these programs. This could include major national certifications for these applications or basic familiarity courses from free training sites, for example, Khan Academy® (https://www.khanacademy.org/) or Udacity® (https://www.udacity.com/).

DOD has not defined the level and type of training for this requirement. It requires privileged users to have an understanding and training certificate (with no specified time length) for the dominant Operating System (OS) the corporate IT infrastructure employs.

MORE COMPLETE ANSWER: If IT personnel have formal certification (such as from a Microsoft ® partner training program), these are ideal artifacts that should be part of the BOE.

ASSESSMENT OBJECTIVE *Determine if:*		
SUB-CTRL	DESCRIPTION	RECOMMENDED APPROACH
3.2.2[a]	*Information security-related duties, roles, and responsibilities are defined.*	NCR
3.2.2[b]	*Information security-related duties, roles, and responsibilities are assigned to designated personnel.*	NCR
3.2.2[c]	*Personnel are adequately trained to carry out their assigned information security-related duties, roles, and responsibilities.*	NCR

Derived Security Requirements:

3.2.3 Provide security awareness training on recognizing and reporting potential indicators of insider threat.

MINIMUM ANSWER: The DOD's Defense Security Service (DSS) in Quantico, VA, is the executive agent for insider threat activities. The DSS provides many training opportunities and toolkits on Insider Threat. These are available from their agency website for free at http://www.dss.mil/it/index.html. This is an excellent resource to create an insider threat training program already developed for the company's use.

Document company minimum training requirements for both general and privileged users, such as watching select online instruction or computer-based training opportunities from DSS. Everyone in the company should participate and satisfactorily complete the training.

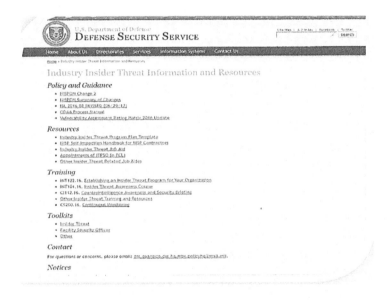

MORE COMPLETE ANSWER: More-complete proof of company compliance with this security control requirement might include guest speakers, or insider threat brown-bag events around lunchtime. Company training personnel should capture attendance records to include sign-in rosters. These could be used for annual training requirements specific to insider threat familiarity.

Also, recommend a **train-the-trainer program** where select individuals are trained by either DSS or other competent company that becomes corporate resources. These assigned individuals could provide both training and first-responder support as needed and be deployed to other company sites.

ASSESSMENT OBJECTIVE *Determine if:*		
SUB-CTRL	DESCRIPTION	RECOMMENDED APPROACH
3.2.3[a]	Potential indicators associated with insider threats are identified.	P-Identify this in association with a Risk Assessment (RA) as described in Control 3.2.2.
3.2.3[b]	Security awareness training on recognizing and reporting potential indicators of insider threat is provided to managers and employees.	NCR

AUDIT AND ACCOUNTABILITY (AU)
System Logs and their Regular Review

The AU control is primarily about the ability of the system owner/company to monitor unauthorized access to the system through system logging functions of the Operating System and other network devices such as firewalls. A System Administrator (SA) is typically assigned the duty to review log files; these may include both authorized and unauthorized access to the network, applications, databases, financial systems, etc. Most businesses will rely on manual review; however, some "smart" servers and firewalls can provide automated alerts to IT personnel of unauthorized use or intrusion. The key is to understand the auditing capabilities of the corporate system and be prepared to defend its capabilities and limitations if DOD representatives or third-party DOD assessors request proof of control compliance.

```
..sion Detection System
.**] [1:1407:9] SNMP trap udp [**]
[Classification: Attempted Information Leak] [Priority: 2]
03/06-8:14:09.082119 192.168.1.167:1052 -> 172.30.128.27:162
UDP TTL:118 TOS:0x0 ID:29101 IpLen:20 DgmLen:87

Personal Firewall
3/6/2006 8:14:07 AM,"Rule ""Block Windows File Sharing"" blocked (192.168.1.54,
netbios-ssn(139)).","Rule ""Block Windows File Sharing"" blocked (192.168.1.54,
netbios-ssn(139)). Inbound TCP connection. Local address,service is
(KENT(172.30.128.27),netbios-ssn(139)). Remote address,service is
(192.168.1.54,39922). Process name is ""System""."

3/3/2006 9:04:04 AM,Firewall configuration updated: 398 rules.,Firewall configuration
updated: 398 rules.

Antivirus Software, Log 1
3/4/2006 9:33:50 AM,Definition File Download,KENT,userk,Definition downloader
3/4/2006 9:33:09 AM,AntiVirus Startup,KENT,userk,System
3/3/2006 3:56:46 PM,AntiVirus Shutdown,KENT,userk,System

Antivirus Software, Log 2
240203071234,16,3,7,KENT,userk,......,16777216,"Virus definitions are
current.",0.,0.,,,,0,,,,,,,,,SAVPROD,{ xxxxxxxx-xxxx-xxxx-xxxx-xxxxxxxxxxxx }.End
User,(IP)-192.168.1.121.,GROUP,0:0:0:0:0,9.0.0.338,,,,,,,,,,,,,

Antispyware Software
DSO Exploit: Data source object exploit (Registry change, nothing done)  HKEY_USERS\S-
1-5-19\Software\Microsoft\Windows\CurrentVersion\Internet Settings\Zones\0\1004!=W=
```

Audit log type examples. The logs above are good examples of the system logs that should be reviewed regularly. These are the business's responsibility to monitor the network actively. Another term of high interest is **Continuous Monitoring (ConMon)**; see the article in Appendix C discussing the importance of ConMon capabilities. Both manual and automated means can accomplish ConMon, and auditing is a significant control family supporting the objectives of this cybersecurity principle.

ConMon activities are best described as the ability of the business to "continuously" monitor the state of its network within its defined security boundary. It should be a capability to determine, for example, who, when, and what are within the

company's security boundary and any reporting requirements in the event of an intrusion. It will be based on the log discovery of unauthorized activities.
(SOURCE: *Guide to Computer Security Log Management*, NIST SP 800-92, September 2006, http://nvlpubs.nist.gov/nistpubs/Legacy/SP/nistspecialpublication800-92.pdf) .

For a greater description of the purpose and components of Continuous Monitoring, see Appendix C: ***Continuous Monitoring: A More Detailed Discussion.***

Basic Security Requirements:

3.3.1 Create, protect, and retain information system audit records to the extent needed to enable the monitoring, analysis, investigation, and reporting of unlawful, unauthorized, or inappropriate information system activity.
MINIMUM ANSWER: The critical part of this control is about audit record retention. The control defines the retention period as a vague capability to retain such records to the most significant "extent possible." The guidance should always be based on the sensitivity of the data. Another consideration should include the ability to provide forensic data to investigators to determine the intrusion over a period.

The historical OPM Breach occurred over several years until OPM even recognized multiple incidents. This included the exfiltration of millions of personnel and security background investigation files. OPM failures, while many, including poor audit processes and review, are a significant factor in the success of nation-state hackers. OPM's poor audit and retention processes made reconstructing critical events more than difficult for government forensics and associated criminal investigations.

The recommendation to small and medium businesses conducting DOD contract activities would be at least one year and preferably two years of audit log retention. Companies should regularly discuss with DOD its specified requirements and should also visit the National Archives Record Agency (NARA) (www.nara.gov) for CUI/CDI data retention as part of an active audit program.

Businesses should always balance operations (and long-term costs) with security (the ability to reconstruct an intrusion, to support law enforcement)

MORE COMPLETE ANSWER: A greater ability to recognize breaches (events and incidents) could include a new internal process and assigned first-responders who would act upon these occurrences. This response team may have additional specialized training to include the use of select network analysis support tools to include packet inspection training using tools such as Wireshark ® (https://www.wireshark.org/).

ASSESSMENT OBJECTIVE *Determine if:*		
SUB-CTRL	*DESCRIPTION*	**RECOMMENDED APPROACH**
3.3.1[a]	*Audit logs needed (i.e., event types to be logged) to enable the monitoring, analysis, investigation, and reporting of unlawful or unauthorized system activity are specified.*	NCR
3.3.1[b]	*The content of audit records needed to support monitoring, analysis, investigation, and reporting of unlawful or unauthorized system activity is defined.*	NCR
3.3.1[c]	*Audit records are created (generated).*	NCR
3.3.1[d]	*Audit records, once created, contain the defined content.*	P - ("Defined content" is too vague. This should at a minimum

			be the login ID [the person], date-time stamp, IP address, MAC address, and all commands executed).
	3.3.1[e]	*Retention requirements for audit records are defined.*	NCR – Refer to National Archives Record Agency (NARA) (www.nara.gov) for CUI/CDI data retention.
	3.3.1[f]	*Audit records are retained as defined.*	NCR

3.3.2 Ensure that the actions of individual information system users can be uniquely traced to those users, so they can be held accountable for their actions.

MINIMUM ANSWER: This is about the capture of individual users as they access the system. Access logs should include, for example, user identification information, timestamps of all access, databases or applications accessed, and some failed login attempts. This control is designed for potential forensic reconstruction for either internal policy violations or external threat intrusions. Any policy considerations should include at least a weekly review, but any audit review periodicity should be based on the sensitivity and criticality of data to the business's overall mission.

MORE COMPLETE ANSWER: A more complete means to address this control is using automated alerts to crucial IT and management personnel. This could include capabilities from existing "smart" firewalls, or more advanced solutions may consist of a **Security Information & Event Management** (SIEM) solution. These are more complicated and expensive solutions, but current developments employing modern Artificial Intelligence and Machine Learning technologies to more proactively identify threats are evolving rapidly; these solutions should be less costly and more comfortable to deploy within the next decade.

ASSESSMENT OBJECTIVE		
Determine if:		
SUB-CTRL	*DESCRIPTION*	RECOMMENDED APPROACH
3.3.2[a]	The content of the audit records needed to support the ability to uniquely trace users to their actions is defined.	NCR
3.3.2[b]	Audit records, once created, contain the defined content.	NCR

Derived Security Requirements:

3.3.3 Review and update audited events.

MINIMUM ANSWER: This is a similar requirement to other AU controls above to regularly review audit logs. We recommend at least weekly reviews.

MORE COMPLETE ANSWER: To more completely address this control, IT personnel could categorize the log types being collected. These could include, for example, Operating System (OS) (network), application, firewall, database logs, etc.

ASSESSMENT OBJECTIVE		
Determine if:		
SUB-CTRL	*DESCRIPTION*	RECOMMENDED APPROACH
3.3.3[a]	A process for determining when to review logged events is defined.	NCR
3.3.3[b]	Event types being logged are reviewed in accordance with the defined review process.	P-"Event types" could include failed logons, file deletions, modifications, or changes (especially in critical databases such as HR or finance).

| 3.3.3[c] | Event types being logged are updated based on the review. | P-(See Above) |

3.3.4 Alert in the event of an audit process failure.

MINIMUM ANSWER: This is an active ability developed within the company's audit technology that can alert personnel of an audit failure.

This could include local alarms, flashing lights, SMS, and email alerts to key company personnel. This will require SA and IT personnel to set policy settings to be established as part of the routine checks in support of the overall audit function and control. A description of the technical implementation and immediate actions to be taken by personnel should be identified. This should include the activation of the Incident Response (IR) Plan.

MORE COMPLETE ANSWER: Additional technical solutions could include supplementary systems to be monitored. This could consist of the state of all audit-capable devices and functions. This may also include a separate computer or a backup auditing server for the storage of logs, not on the primary system; this would prevent intruders from deleting or changing logs to hide their presence in the network.

These solutions will ultimately add additional complexity and cost. Ensure any solution is supportable both financially and technically by company decision-makers. While to have greater security is an overall desire of the NIST 800-171 implementation, it should be balanced with a practical and measurable value-added approach to adding any new technologies. It should also be a further consideration that the incorporation of new technologies should address the impacts of added complexity and determining the ability of IT support personnel to maintain it.

ASSESSMENT OBJECTIVE *Determine if:*		
SUB-CTRL	*DESCRIPTION*	**RECOMMENDED APPROACH**
3.3.4[a]	*Personnel or roles to be alerted in the event of an audit logging process failure are identified.*	NCR

3.3.4[b]	Types of audit logging process failures for which alert will be generated are defined.	NCR
3.3.4[c]	Identified personnel or roles are alerted in the event of an audit logging process failure.	NCR

3.3.5 Correlate audit review, analysis, and reporting processes for investigation and response to indications of inappropriate, suspicious, or unusual activity.

MINIMUM ANSWER: This should identify the technical actions taken by authorized audit personnel to pursue when analyzing suspicious activity on the network.

It should also be tied to the IR Plan and be tested at least annually. (See Control IR for further discussion of **DOD Precedence Identification** and determine actions based on the level of severity).

MORE COMPLETE ANSWER: See Control 3.3.2 for a more detailed discussion of employing a SIEM solution. In addition to manual analysis, the company could leverage the capabilities of newer threat identification technologies such as SIEM and "smart" Intrusion Detection and Prevention devices.

ASSESSMENT OBJECTIVE Determine if:		
SUB-CTRL	DESCRIPTION	RECOMMENDED APPROACH
3.3.5[a]	Audit record review, analysis, and reporting processes for investigation and response to indications of unlawful, unauthorized, suspicious, or unusual activity are defined.	NCR
3.3.5[b]	Defined audit record review, analysis, and reporting processes are correlated.	NCR

3.3.6 Provide audit reduction and report generation to support on-demand analysis and reporting.

MINIMUM ANSWER: Audit reduction provides for "on-demand" audit review, analysis, and reporting requirements.

This should at least use manual methods to collect audits from across multiple audit logging devices to assist with potential forensic needs. Any procedural effort to support audit reduction most likely can use commercial support applications and scripts (small programs typically are explicitly written to the business's unique IT environment) that IT personnel should be able to assist in their identification, development, and procurement.

MORE COMPLETE ANSWER: IT personnel could identify more automated and integrated audit reduction solutions. Likely candidates could be "smart" firewalls or Security Information and Event Management (SIEM) solutions.

ASSESSMENT OBJECTIVE *Determine if:*		
SUB-CTRL	DESCRIPTION	RECOMMENDED APPROACH
3.3.6[a]	An audit record reduction capability that supports on-demand analysis is provided.	NCR (if required to automate then a POAM or Waiver may be necessary)
3.3.6[b]	A report generation capability that supports on-demand reporting is provided.	NCR (This could be as basic as a data-run to provide ad hoc reporting requests).

3.3.7 Provide an information system capability that compares and synchronizes internal system clocks with an authoritative source to generate timestamps for audit records.

MINIMUM ANSWER: The most straightforward answer is to have IT personnel use the Network Time Protocol (NTP) on **NTP port 123** to provide US Naval Observatory timestamps as the standard for the network. This is used as the authoritative source within DOD. The system clocks of all processors (computers, firewalls, etc.) within the company should be set to the same time when first initialized by IT support staff; this should be an explicit policy requirement.

It is suggested that SA personnel review and compare the external (NTP server time stamp) with internal system clocks. This can be used to identify log changes if synchronization is not the same from the external and internal clock settings. Log changes may be an indicator of unauthorized access and manipulation of log files by hackers.

MORE COMPLETE ANSWER: Several automated programs can be used, and good basic programmers within the company could write scripts (small pieces of executable code) to provide these comparisons more easily.

ASSESSMENT OBJECTIVE *Determine if:*		
SUB-CTRL	*DESCRIPTION*	**RECOMMENDED APPROACH**
3.3.7[a]	Internal system clocks are used to generate timestamps for audit records.	P-The control here is calling for relying on "internal" clocks; BE AWARE hackers can manipulate system clocks.
3.3.7[b]	An authoritative source with which to compare and synchronize internal system clocks is specified.	NCR
3.3.7[c]	Internal system clocks used to generate timestamps for audit records are compared to and synchronized with the specified authoritative time source.	NCR

3.3.8 Protect audit information and audit tools from unauthorized access, modification, and deletion.

MINIMUM ANSWER: This control requires greater protection of audit files and auditing tools from unauthorized users. These tools can be exploited by intruders to change log files or delete them entirely to hide their entry into the system. Password protect and limit use to only authorized personnel. Document this process accordingly.

MORE COMPLETE ANSWER: This information could be stored in some other server, not part of the normal audit log capture area. Additionally, conduct regular backups to prevent intruders from manipulating logs; this will allow a means to compare changes, and identify potential incidents in the network for action by senior management or law enforcement.

ASSESSMENT OBJECTIVE *Determine if:*		
SUB-CTRL	*DESCRIPTION*	*RECOMMENDED APPROACH*
3.3.8[a]	Audit information is protected from unauthorized access.	NCR
3.3.8[b]	Audit information is protected from unauthorized modification.	NCR
3.3.8[c]	Audit information is protected from unauthorized deletion.	NCR
3.3.8[d]	Audit logging tools are protected from unauthorized access.	NCR
3.3.8[e]	Audit logging tools are protected from unauthorized modification.	NCR
3.3.8[f]	Audit logging tools are protected from unauthorized deletion.	NCR

3.3.9 Limit management of audit functionality to a subset of privileged users.
MINIMUM ANSWER: See Control 3.3.8 for reducing the numbers of personnel with access to audit logs and functions. Maintaining a roster of staff with appropriate user agreements can afford the ability to limit personnel as well as provide value in any future forensic activities required.

MORE COMPLETE ANSWER: Several products such as CyberArk ® could be used to manage and monitor privileged user access to audit information. This product will be a relatively expensive solution for small and some medium-sized businesses.

ASSESSMENT OBJECTIVE Determine if:		
SUB-CTRL	*DESCRIPTION*	**RECOMMENDED APPROACH**
3.3.9[a]	*A subset of privileged users granted access to manage audit logging functionality is defined.*	NCR
3.3.9[b]	*Management of audit logging functionality is limited to the defined subset of privileged users.*	NCR

CONFIGURATION MANAGEMENT (CM)
The True Foundation of Cybersecurity

The real importance of Configuration Management is it is, in fact, the "opposite side of the same coin" called cybersecurity. CM is used to track and confirm changes to the system's baseline; this could be changed in hardware, firmware, and software that would alert IT professionals to unauthorized modifications to the IT environment. CM is used to confirm and ensure programmatic controls prevent changes that have not been adequately tested or approved.

CM requires establishing baselines for tracking, controlling, and managing a business's internal IT infrastructure specific to NIST 800-171. Companies with an effective CM process need to consider information security implications for the development and operation of information systems. This will include the active management of changes to company hardware, software, and documentation.

Effective CM of information systems requires the integration of the management of secure configurations into the CM process. If good CM exists as a well-defined "change" process, the protection of the IT environment is more assured. This should be considered as the second most important security control. It is suggested that both management and IT personnel have adequate knowledge and training to maintain this process since it is so integral to good programmatic and cybersecurity practice.

Basic Security Requirements:

3.4.1 Establish and maintain baseline configurations and inventories of organizational information systems (including hardware, software, firmware, and documentation) throughout the respective system development life cycles.
MINIMUM ANSWER: This control can be best met by hardware, software, and firmware (should be combined with hardware) listings; these are the classic artifacts required for any system within the DOD. Updating these documents as changes to the IT architecture is both a critical IT and logistics' functions. Ensure these staffs are well-coordinated about system changes. ***This should be included in the System Security Plan (SSP).***

Also, NIST 800-171 requires document control of all reports, documents, manuals, etc. The currency of all related documents should be managed in a centralized repository.

Where documents may be sensitive, such as describing existing weaknesses or vulnerabilities of the IT infrastructure, these documents should have a higher level of control. The rationale for greater control of such documents is if these documents were "found" in the public, hackers, or Advanced Persistent Threats (i.e., adversarial nation-states) could use this information to conduct exploits. Vulnerabilities about company systems should be marked and controlled, at least at the CUI/CDI level.

MORE COMPLETE ANSWER: Suggested better approaches to exercising good **version control** activities would be using a shared network drive, or a more advanced solution could use Microsoft ® SharePoint ®. An active version control tool should only allow authorized personnel to make changes to critical documents and system changes and their associated **versioning**—significant changes within the IT architecture, for example, from version 2.0 to 3.0. This should also maintain audit records of who and when a file is accessed and modified.

ASSESSMENT OBJECTIVE *Determine if:*		
SUB-CTRL	**DESCRIPTION**	**RECOMMENDED APPROACH**
3.4.1[a]	A baseline configuration is established.	NCR(SSP) The SSP is the defined artifact to capture such information
3.4.1[b]	The baseline configuration includes hardware, software, firmware, and documentation.	NCR(SSP)
3.4.1[c]	The baseline configuration is maintained (reviewed and updated) throughout the system development life cycle.	P-Need to define and update as changes in configuration occur. Who or what body updates and maintains the "baseline" specific to the SSP
3.4.1[d]	A system inventory is established.	NCR(SSP)
3.4.1[e]	The system inventory includes hardware, software, firmware, and documentation.	NCR(SSP)
3.4.1[f]	The inventory is maintained (reviewed and updated)	P-See Sub-control 3.4.1[c]

| | | *throughout the system development life cycle.* | |

3.4.2 Establish and enforce security configuration settings for information technology products employed in organizational information systems.

MINIMUM/MORE COMPLETE ANSWER: There should be an identification of any security configuration settings in the business's procedural documents. This would include technical policy settings, for example, the number of failed logins, minimum password length, mandatory logoff settings, etc. These settings should be identified by a company's Operating System, software application, or program.

ASSESSMENT OBJECTIVE *Determine if:*		
SUB-CTRL	***DESCRIPTION***	**RECOMMENDED APPROACH**
3.4.2[a]	*Security configuration settings for information technology products employed in the system are established and included in the baseline configuration.*	P- *"Security configuration settings for information technology products employed in the system are established and included in the baseline configuration."*
3.4.2[b]	*Security configuration settings for information technology products employed in the system are enforced.*	P- *"Security configuration settings for information technology products employed in the system are enforced."*

Derived Security Requirements:

3.4.3 Track, review, approve/disapprove, and audit changes to information systems.

MINIMUM ANSWER: This control addresses a defined corporate change *process*. This should be able to add or remove IT components within the network and provide needed currency regarding the state of the network. This should not be a purely IT staff function. If the firm can afford additional infrastructure personnel, it should assign a configuration manager; this person would administer the CM process.

MORE COMPLETE ANSWER: This could use Commercial Off the Shelf Technologies (COTS) that could be used to establish a more sophisticated CM database. This could also afford a more capable audit ability to prevent unauthorized changes.

ASSESSMENT OBJECTIVE *Determine if:*		
SUB-CTRL	**DESCRIPTION**	**RECOMMENDED APPROACH**
3.4.3[a]	*Changes to the system are tracked.*	NCR
3.4.3[b]	*Changes to the system are reviewed.*	NCR
3.4.3[c]	*Changes to the system are approved or disapproved.*	NCR
3.4.3[d]	*Changes to the system are logged.*	NCR

3.4.4 Analyze the security impact of changes prior to implementation.
MINIMUM ANSWER: Under DOD's risk management process, it requires that any changes to the baseline necessitate some level of technical analysis. This analysis is described as a **Security Impact Analysis (SIA),** and it is looking for any positive or negative changes that are considered **security-relevant**.

This analysis should look at any change to the architecture, be it changes in hardware, software, firmware, or architecture. This should be described in the corporate CM process and could be as basic as a write-up from a member of the IT team, for example, that the change will or will not have a security impact, and it may or may not be security-relevant.

If the change introduces a "negative" impact, such as eliminating backup capabilities or adding currently unsupportable software (possibly due to funding constraints)**, it is the responsibility of the company to reinitiate the NIST 800-171 process in-full and advise DOD of the rationale for the change.**

See CM control 3.4.4 for a detailed Decision-tree.

MORE COMPLETE ANSWER: A more-complete solution to this control would include, for example, the addition of a new software product that supports vulnerability scans using corporate anti-virus and malware applications or software products. Attach these reports as part of the record.

In the case of hardware updates, the company could demonstrate its SCRM process by attaching proof that the manufacturer is an authorized vendor approved by the DOD. Access to DOD's Approved Products List (APL) may require the Contracting Officer Representative (COR) or Contracting Officer (CO) to approve access to DOD databases maintained by the Defense Information Systems Agency (DISA) at Fort Meade, MD. It most likely will only allow a limited number of company personnel to be issued DOD CAC "tokens" to access these sites; the positive review of these databases will demonstrate the proper level of due diligence for any current or future Authorization to Operate (ATO).

3.4.5 Define, document, approve, and enforce physical and logical access restrictions associated with changes to the information system.

MINIMUM/MORE COMPLETE ANSWER: "Access restrictions" are aligned with the earlier discussed AC controls. As part of a corporate CM policy, any changes to the IT baseline needs to be captured within a formal process approved by that process and documented. Documentation is typically maintained in a CM database, and more specifically, it would require the update of any hardware or software lists. Proof of compliance would be the production of updated listings that are maintained by the CM database. This should include the updating of any network diagrams describing in a graphic form a description of the corporate network; these are all explicit requirements under NIST 800-171. These artifacts should also be included in the **SSP**.

ASSESSMENT OBJECTIVE *Determine if:*		
SUB-CTRL	*DESCRIPTION*	**RECOMMENDED APPROACH**
3.4.5[a]	*Physical access restrictions associated with changes to the system are defined.*	NCR

3.4.5[b]	*Physical access restrictions associated with changes to the system are documented.*	NCR
3.4.5[c]	*Physical access restrictions associated with changes to the system are approved.*	NCR
3.4.5[d]	*Physical access restrictions associated with changes to the system are enforced.*	NCR
3.4.5[e]	*Logical access restrictions associated with changes to the system are defined.*	NCR-("Logical access" is described under Access Control is full).
3.4.5[f]	*Logical access restrictions associated with changes to the system are documented.*	NCR
3.4.5[g]	*Logical access restrictions associated with changes to the system are approved.*	NCR
3.4.5[h]	*Logical access restrictions associated with changes to the system are enforced.*	NCR

3.4.6 Employ the principle of least functionality by configuring the information system to provide only essential capabilities.

MINIMUM ANSWER: The DOD has defined the use, for example, of File Transfer Protocol (FTP), Bluetooth, or peer-to-peer networking as insecure protocols. These protocols are unauthorized within DOD environments, and companies seeking NIST 800-171 approval are best to follow this direction as well. Any written procedure should attempt to at least annually reassess whether a determination of the security of all functions, ports, protocols, or services are still correct.

MORE COMPLETE ANSWER: The use of automated network packet tools is recommended to conduct such reassessments. Ensure that IT personnel have the right experience and skill to provide a proper analysis of this control requirement.

ASSESSMENT OBJECTIVE Determine if:		
SUB-CTRL	DESCRIPTION	RECOMMENDED APPROACH
3.4.6[a]	Essential system capabilities are defined based on the principle of least functionality.	NCR-(See earlier discussion regarding conducting an initial and annual Risk Assessment (RA))
3.4.6[b]	The system is configured to provide only the defined essential capabilities.	NCR

3.4.7 Restrict, disable, and prevent the use of nonessential programs, functions, ports, protocols, and services.

MINIMUM ANSWER: Nonessential programs, functions, ports, and protocols are prime attack avenues for would-be hackers. Any programs that are not used for the conduct of business operations should be removed. Where that is not possible, these programs should be blacklisted to run in the company's IT environment. (See 3.4.8. below).

Regarding ports and protocols, this will require IT staff direct involvement in the decision-making process. Specific ports are typically needed for any 21st Century company's daily operation. For example, ports 80, 8080, and 443 are used to send HTTP (web traffic); these ports will typically be required to be active.

Port Number	Application Supported
20	File Transport Protocol (FTP) Data
23	Telnet
25	Simple Mail Transfer Protocol (SMTP)
80, 8080, 443	Hypertext Transport Protocol (HTTP) → WWW
110	Post Office Protocol version 3 (POP3)

Common Ports and Their Associated Protocols

For those ports and protocols that are not required, they should be closed by designated IT personnel. This prevents hackers from exploiting open entries into the corporate infrastructure. Ensure a copy of all open and closed ports is readily available to DOD representatives for review as part of the NIST 800-171 requirements.

MORE COMPLETE ANSWER: The business could employ tools that check for unused and open ports. This could include a regular reassessment of whether ports need to remain active. As mentioned earlier, products such as Wireshark ® could be used as a low-cost solution to conduct any reassessment of the corporate infrastructure.

ASSESSMENT OBJECTIVE *Determine if:*		
SUB-CTRL	*DESCRIPTION*	RECOMMENDED APPROACH
3.4.7[a]	*Essential programs are defined.*	NCR (Always consult with Contract Office to determine any specified unauthorized programs, for example, "hacker tools," etc.
3.4.7[b]	*The use of nonessential programs is defined.*	NCR
3.4.7[c]	*The use of nonessential programs is restricted, disabled, or prevented as defined.*	NCR
3.4.7[d]	*Essential functions are defined.*	NCR (artifact would include all "whitelisted" applications and functions)
3.4.7[e]	*The use of nonessential functions is defined.*	NCR
3.4.7[f]	*The use of nonessential functions is restricted, disabled, or prevented as defined.*	NCR
3.4.7[g]	*Essential ports are defined.*	NCR (Coordinate with Contract office at least annually regarding any

		updates to unauthorized ports).
3.4.7[h]	The use of nonessential ports is defined.	NCR
3.4.7[i]	The use of nonessential ports is restricted, disabled, or prevented as defined.	NCR
3.4.7[j]	Essential protocols are defined.	NCR (Same as 3.4.7[g])
3.4.7[k]	The use of nonessential protocols is defined.	NCR
3.4.7[l]	The use of nonessential protocols is restricted, disabled, or prevented as defined.	NCR
3.4.7[m]	Essential services are defined.	NCR (Same as 3.4.7[g])
3.4.7[n]	The use of nonessential services is defined.	NCR
3.4.7[o]	The use of nonessential services is restricted, disabled, or prevented as defined.	NCR

3.4.8 Apply deny-by-exception (blacklist) policy to prevent the use of unauthorized software or deny all, permit-by-exception (whitelisting) policy to allow the execution of authorized software.

MINIMUM/MORE COMPLETE ANSWER: The company should employ **blacklisting** or **whitelisting,** (See Control 3.14.2 for more information), to prohibit the execution of unauthorized software programs or applications within the information system. A copy of the current listing should be part of the formal Body of Evidence (BOE).

| ASSESSMENT OBJECTIVE
Determine if:		
SUB-CTRL	*DESCRIPTION*	**RECOMMENDED APPROACH**
3.4.8[a]	*A policy specifying whether whitelisting or blacklisting is to be implemented is specified.*	NCR
3.4.8[b]	*The software allowed to execute under whitelisting or denied use under blacklisting is specified.*	NCR
3.4.8[c]	*Whitelisting to allow the execution of authorized software or blacklisting to prevent the use of unauthorized software is implemented as specified.*	NCR

3.4.9 Control and monitor user-installed software.

MINIMUM ANSWER: The policy should always be that only authorized administrators, such as designated SA's and senior help desk personnel, be allowed to add or delete the software from user computers.

There should also be a defined process to request specialized software to be added for unique users. These may include finance personnel, architects, statisticians, etc. that require specialized stand-alone software that may or may not connect to the Internet.

MORE COMPLETE ANSWER: This could include as part of the company's normal audit process the review of whether personnel is adding software and bypassing security measures (such as getting passwords from IT authorized individuals). This may also be addressed in the AUP and supported by appropriate HR activities that can be pursued against individuals of any such violations.

ASSESSMENT OBJECTIVE *Determine if:*		
SUB-CTRL	*DESCRIPTION*	**RECOMMENDED APPROACH**
3.4.9[a]	*A policy for controlling the installation of software by users is established.*	NCR
3.4.9[b]	*Installation of software by users is controlled based on the established policy.*	NCR
3.4.9[c]	*Installation of software by users is monitored.*	NCR

IDENTIFICATION AND AUTHENTICATION (IA)
Why is two-factor authentication so important?

The 2015 Office of Personnel Management (OPM) breach could have been prevented if this control family was adequately implemented and enforced. The one positive effect that the OPM breach produced for DOD and other federal agencies was the explicit requirement from Congress that these requirements became mandatory. Congress's focus on the use of Two-Factor Authentication (2FA) and Multi-Factor Authentication (MFA) has provided positive results for the federal government and impetus for more stringent cybersecurity measures beyond the government's IT boundaries.

While some businesses will be afforded, for example, Common Access Cards (CAC) to accomplish 2FA between the company and DOD, most will not be authorized such access. Implementation will require various levels of investment, and the use of 2FA devices, or also called "tokens." This, too, will require additional financial costs and technical integration challenges for the average business.

For many small businesses, this will require some sizeable investment on the part of the company and a clear commitment to working with the DOD. Solutions could include, for example, RSA® tokens—these are small devices that regularly rotate a security variable (a key) that a user enters in addition to a password or Personal Identification Number (PIN). This solution affords one potential solution to businesses to meet the 2FA requirement.

According to The House Committee on Oversight and Government Reform report on September 7th, 2016, OPM's leadership failed to "implement basic cyber hygiene, such as maintaining current authorities to operate <u>and employing strong multi-factor authentication</u>, despite years of warning from the Inspector General... tools were available that could have prevented the breaches..." (SOURCE: <u>https://oversight.house.gov/wp-content/uploads/2016/09/The-OPM-Data-Breach-How-the-Government-Jeopardized-Our-National-Security-for-More-than-a-Generation.pdf</u>)

The best approaches will require good market surveys of the available resources and be mindful that two-factor do not need to be a card or token solution. Other options would include biometrics (fingerprints, facial recognition, etc.) or Short Message Service (SMS) 2FA solution as used by Amazon® to verify its customers. They use a Two-Step verification process that provides a "verification code sent to the customer's personal cell phone or home phone to verify their identity.

Be prepared to do serious "homework" on these controls and research all potential solutions. Once this control is resolved, the company will be in a better position not just with DOD but have serious answers that will ensure the protection of its sensitive data.

Basic Security Requirements:

3.5.1 Identify information system users, processes acting on behalf of users, or devices.

MINIMUM/MORE COMPLETE ANSWER: This control should identify/reference current business procedures as outlined in the **AU** control above. It should address that audit is used to identify system users, the processes (applications), and the devices (computers) accessed.

ASSESSMENT OBJECTIVE *Determine if:*		
SUB-CTRL	**DESCRIPTION**	**RECOMMENDED APPROACH**
3.5.1[a]	System users are identified.	NCR
3.5.1[b]	Processes acting on behalf of users are identified.	NCR (through audit log collection)
3.5.1[c]	Devices accessing the system are identified.	NCR

3.5.2 Authenticate (or verify) the identities of those users, processes, or devices, as a prerequisite to allowing access to organizational information systems.
MINIMUM ANSWER: While basic logon and password information could be used, Control 3.5.3 below, requires Multifactor or Two-factor Authentication (2FA). DOD requires 2FA, and NIST 800-171 requires it.

Remember, if the company is not immediately prepared to execute a 2FA solution, *a POAM is required*.

MORE COMPLETE ANSWER: The better answer is the employment of some form of 2FA. It could be a **hard token** solution such as a CAC or PIV card. The other option would include such virtual solutions that would use email or SMS messaging like Google ® or Amazon ® to provide 2FA; this **soft token** solution is typically easier and less expensive to deploy. It can be more easily used to meet this DOD and NIST 800-171 requirement.

ASSESSMENT OBJECTIVE *Determine if:*		
SUB-CTRL	*DESCRIPTION*	**RECOMMENDED APPROACH**
3.5.2[a]	*The identity of each user is authenticated or verified as a prerequisite to system access.*	NCR
3.5.2[b]	*The identity of each process acting on behalf of a user is authenticated or verified as a prerequisite to system access.*	NCR
3.5.2[c]	*The identity of each device accessing or connecting to the system is authenticated or verified as a prerequisite to system access.*	P/T/PO/W- This will require policy and potential technical control updates where, for example, servers are authenticating to other servers securely. This may require a POAM or waiver in certain time-restricted circumstances.

Derived Security Requirements:

3.5.3 Use multifactor authentication for local and network access to privileged accounts and for network access to non-privileged accounts.

MINIMUM ANSWER: See Control 3.5.2 above. Ensure the requirement for MFA or 2FA is part of the company's cybersecurity policy/procedure.

MORE COMPLETE ANSWER: (See Control 3.5.2 for suggested approaches).

ASSESSMENT OBJECTIVE *Determine if:*		
SUB-CTRL	DESCRIPTION	RECOMMENDED APPROACH
3.5.3[a]	*Privileged accounts are identified.*	NCR
3.5.3[b]	*Multifactor authentication is implemented for local access to privileged accounts.*	NCR (At least two-factor authentication; Windows 10® allows for biometric facial recognition—a potential small architecture solution for many)
3.5.3[c]	*Multifactor authentication is implemented for network access to privileged accounts.*	NCR
3.5.3[d]	*Multifactor authentication is implemented for network access to non-privileged accounts.*	NCR

3.5.4 Employ replay-resistant authentication mechanisms for network access to privileged and nonprivileged accounts.

MINIMUM ANSWER: This control requires replay-resistant technologies to prevent replay attacks. **Replay attacks** are also known as a **playback attack**. This is an attack where the hacker captures legitimate traffic from an authorized user, and presumably a positively identified network user, and uses it to gain unauthorized access to a network. This is also considered a form of a **Man-in-the-Middle** type attack.

The most natural solution to resolving this control is to have company IT personnel disable **Secure Socket Layer (SSL)**—which DOD no longer authorizes. Businesses should use the **Transport Layer Security (TLS) 2.0** or higher; it as a required DOD standard.

If the business needs to continue the use of SSL to maintain connectivity with, for example, external or third-party data providers, a POAM is required. Efforts should be made to discuss with these data providers when they will no longer be using SSL. This discussion should begin as soon as possible to advise DOD through a POAM that demonstrates the company is conducting its proper due diligence to protect its CUI/CDI.

MORE COMPLETE ANSWER: A potentially expensive solution could include the addition of a **SIEM** solution. Many major IT network providers have added artificial intelligence capabilities to detect this type of attack better; identify any solution carefully.

3.5.5 Prevent reuse of identifiers for a defined period.

MINIMUM ANSWER: This IA control directs that "individual, group, role, or device identifiers" from being reused. This should be included as part of any written procedure and defined in system policies to prevent identifiers from being reused. This could consist of email address names (individual), administrator accounts (group), or device identifiers such as "finan_db" designating a high-value target such as a "financial database" (device).

The reason for this control is to prevent intruders who have gained information about such identifiers having less of a capability to use this information for an exploit of the business. This will help better thwart hacker's intelligence collection and analysis of a company's internal network. This control is designed to prevent intruders' abilities to gain access to corporate systems and their resident CUI/CDI repositories.

MORE COMPLETE ANSWER: Reuse of individual identifiers should be discouraged, for example, in the case of a returning employee. This is an essential suggestion: 'John.Smith@cui-company.com' could be varied examples, 'John.H.Smith2@cui-company.com.

ASSESSMENT OBJECTIVE *Determine if:*		
SUB-CTRL	DESCRIPTION	RECOMMENDED APPROACH
3.5.5[a]	A period within which identifiers cannot be reused is defined.	NCR
3.5.5[b]	Reuse of identifiers is prevented within the defined period.	NCR

3.5.6 Disable identifiers after a defined period of inactivity.

MINIMUM/MORE COMPLETE ANSWER: This requires that after a defined time-out setting, the system terminates its connection. The recommendation is 30 minutes maximum, but as mentioned earlier, the time-out should always be based on data sensitivity.

ASSESSMENT OBJECTIVE *Determine if:*		
SUB-CTRL	DESCRIPTION	RECOMMENDED APPROACH
3.5.6[a]	A period of inactivity, after which an identifier is disabled is defined.	NCR
3.5.6[b]	Identifiers are disabled after the defined period of inactivity.	NCR

3.5.7 Enforce a minimum password complexity and change of characters when new passwords are created.

MINIMUM ANSWER: If using passwords for authentication purposes, the expectation is that a POAM has been developed until such time a 2FA or MFA solution is in place. The standard complexity is supposed to be at least 15 characters that include at least two or more alpha, numeric, and special characters to reduce the likelihood of compromise.

MORE COMPLETE ANSWER: Automated policy settings of the network can enforce increased length and variability. Another suggestion is to use passphrases. These can be harder to "crack" by standard hacking tools and are typically easier for users to memorize.

 The best solutions are <u>still</u> either 2FA or MFA.

The factors:
1. Something you know (e.g., password/PIN)
2. Something you have (e.g., cryptographic identification device, token)
3. Something you are (e.g., biometric: fingerprint, iris, etc.).

ASSESSMENT OBJECTIVE *Determine if:*		
SUB-CTRL	**DESCRIPTION**	**RECOMMENDED APPROACH**
3.5.7[a]	*Password complexity requirements are defined.*	NCR
3.5.7[b]	*Password change of character requirements are defined.*	NCR
3.5.7[c]	*Minimum password complexity requirements, as defined are enforced when new passwords are created.*	NCR (Consult with Contract Office specific to DOD's 15-character alpha-numeric requirement)
3.5.7[d]	*Minimum password change of character requirements as defined are enforced when new passwords are created.*	NCR

3.5.8 Prohibit password reuse for a specified number of generations.

MINIMUM ANSWER: This is usually set by policy and the designated SA's that limit the number of times a password can be reused; **passwords within DOD are required to be changed every 90 days.** This function should be automated by authorized IT personnel. Suggested reuse of a prior password should be at least ten or greater

MORE COMPLETE ANSWER: Technical settings can be established for *no* reuse. This ensures that hackers who may have exploited one of the user's other businesses or even (and more especially) personal accounts can be less likely to be effective against corporate computer networks and assets.

ASSESSMENT OBJECTIVE *Determine if:*		
SUB-CTRL	**DESCRIPTION**	**RECOMMENDED APPROACH**
3.5.8[a]	*The number of generations during which a password cannot be reused is specified.*	NCR
3.5.8[b]	*Reuse of passwords is prohibited during the specified number of generations.*	NCR

3.5.9 Allow temporary password use for system logons with an immediate change to a permanent password.

MINIMUM/MORE COMPLETE ANSWER: This setting is typically built into standard network operating systems. This requirement for users should be appropriately included in the recommended procedure guide.

3.5.10 Store and transmit only encrypted representation of passwords.

MINIMUM ANSWER: This is both a DIT and DAR issue. See Control 3.1.3 for a conceptual diagram. IT personnel should be regularly verifying that password data stores are always encrypted.

This control requires that all passwords are encrypted and approved by NIST's sanctioned process under FIPS 140-2. See Control 3.13.11 for the NIST website to confirm whether a cryptographic solution is recommended.

MORE COMPLETE ANSWER: Suggested greater protections could require encrypted passwords that are not collocated on the same main application or database server that stores significant portions of the business's data repository. A separate server (physical or virtual) could prevent hackers from exploits from accessing company data stores.

ASSESSMENT OBJECTIVE *Determine if:*		
SUB-CTRL	*DESCRIPTION*	**RECOMMENDED APPROACH**
3.5.10[a]	*Passwords are cryptographically protected in storage.*	NCR
3.5.10[b]	*Passwords are cryptographically protected in transit.*	NCR

3.5.11. Obscure feedback of authentication information.

MINIMUM/MORE COMPLETE ANSWER: This is like **pattern hiding,** as described in Control 3.1.10. The system should prevent unauthorized individuals from compromising system-level authentication by inadvertently observing in-person ("shoulder surfing") or virtually (by viewing password entries by privileged users) remotely. It relies upon obscuring the "feedback of authentication information," for example, displaying asterisks (*) or hash symbols (#) when a user types their password. This setting should be enforced automatically and prevent general users from changing this setting.

INCIDENT RESPONSE (IR)
What do you do when you are attacked?

Incident Response (IR) primarily requires a plan, an identification of who or what agency is notified when a breach has occurred, and testing of the plan over time. This control requires the development of an Incident Response Plan (IRP). There are many templates available online, and if there is an existing relationship with a DOD agency, companies should be able to get an agency-specific template.

OCCURRENCE →
EVENT (initial observation of potential problem) →
INCIDENT (defined/confirmed/high impact)

Incident Response Spectrum

The first effort should be identifying with DOD representatives what constitutes a reportable event that formally becomes an incident. This could include a confirmed breach that has occurred to the IT infrastructure. Incidents could include anything from a Denial of Service (DOS) attack—overloading of outwardly facing web or mail servers-- or exfiltration of data—where CUI/CDI and corporate data has been copied or moved to outside of the company's firewall/perimeter. Incidents could also include the destruction of data that the company's IT staff, for example, identifies through ongoing audit activities.

Secondarily, who do you notify? Do you alert your assigned Contract Officer Representative (COR), the Contract Office, DOD's US Cybercommand at Fort Meade, MD, or possibly the Department of Homeland Security's (DHS) Computer Emergency Response Team (CERT) (https://www.us-cert.gov/forms/report)? Company representatives will have to ask their assigned COR where to file standard DOD "incident" reports. They should be able to provide templates and forms specific to the DOD agency.

Finally, this security control will require testing at least *annually*, but more often is recommended. Until comfortable with the IR "reporting chain," *practice, practice, practice*.

Cyber Incident Life Cycle. This diagram will assist in approaching the IR activity, and will better assist in coordination with DOD cybersecurity incident response organizations. Recognizing this as either an "event" (not necessarily a negative occurrence) versus an "incident" is an internal call by the company's leadership in coordination with its security and IT professional staff. An incident specifically requires alerting DOD as soon as the intrusion is ***recognized***.

Verify with the respective DOD agency its reporting standards. Typically, **events** need to be reported within 24 hours upon recognition, and **incidents** immediately upon recognition. Always verify this with the assigned COR.

The chart below categorizes the current DOD precedence.

Precedence	Category	Description
0	0	Training and Exercises
1	1	Root Level Intrusion (Incident)
2	2	User Level Intrusion (Incident)
3	4	Denial of Service (Incident)
4	7	Malicious Logic (Incident)
5	3	Unsuccessful Activity Attempt (Event)
6	5	Non-Compliance Activity (Event)
7	6	Reconnaissance (Event)
8	8	Investigating (Event)
9	9	Explained Anomaly (Event)

DOD Precedence Categorization. Nine (9) is the lowest event where little is known, and IT personnel are attempting to determine whether this activity should be elevated to alert company leadership or to "close it out." One (1) is a deep attack. It identifies that the incident has gained "root" access. This level of an incident is critical since an intruder has nearly unlimited access to the network and its data. (SOURCE: CYBER INCIDENT HANDLING PROGRAM, CJCSM 6510.01B, 18 December 2014, http://www.jcs.mil/Portals/36/Documents/Library/Manuals/m651001.pdf?ver=2016-02-05-175710-897)

Basic Security Requirements:

3.6.1 Establish an operational incident-handling capability for organizational information systems that includes adequate preparation, detection, analysis, containment, recovery, and user response activities.

MINIMUM ANSWER: This control addresses a "capability" that needs to be established to respond to events and incidents within the firm's IT security boundary.

This should include the **People, Process, and Technology (PPT) Model** as a recommended guide for answering many of the controls within NIST 800-171. While solutions will not necessarily require a technological answer, consideration of the people (e.g., who? what skill sets? etc.) and process (e.g., notifications to senior management, action workflows, etc.) will meet many of the response requirements.

Use the Cyber Incident **Life Cycle** above to guide the company's operational incident-handling artifact/procedure. This should be an annex to the **SSP**. (See System Security Plan (SSP) Template and Workbook: A Supplement to *DOD NIST 800-171 Compliance Guidebook* on Amazon®). The PPT Model can be used to guide and formulate the IRP annex. A suggested approach is described below, and includes the kinds of questions that should be answered to demonstrate best how best to develop a good IRP:

- Preparation
    - People: Who will perform the action or activity? Training needed? Skill sets?
    - Process: Training policies for cybersecurity and IT professionals to support the IRP
    - Technology: What technology already exists to support IR? What technologies are needed?

- Detection
    - People: Are IT staff able to use audit tools properly to detect intrusions?
    - Process: What are 'best practice' approaches to detect intrusions? Monitor firewall logs? Monitor user activity?
    - Technology: Is the technology's data library current? Are automatic updates enabled?

- Analysis
    - People: Are IT staff capable of doing the analysis required? Can they determine false positive activity?
    - Process: What is the process leadership wants to get useful and actionable data from IT staff? What are the demands for immediate and final reporting timelines?
    - Technology: Are the right tools on-site? Can open-source/web solutions useful? Can DOD or DHS provide valuable data feeds to remain current of threats?

- Containment
    - People: Can IT staff stop the ongoing attack? Do they require additional coding scripting skills to build/update firewall policies?
    - Process: Is the containment process effective? Is allowing the attack to continue to identify the threat entity/location a good idea (to support law enforcement)?
    - Technology: Can software tools quarantine and stop a malware attack? Is shutting down all external connections an excellent immediate solution (at the firewall)?

- Recovery Actions
    - People: Can the IT staff recover backup data files and media?
    - Process: What is the order of recovery? Bring up internal databases and communications first, and external servers (email and web site) be reestablished later? What are the recovery time standards for the company to regain business operations? What is acceptable? What is not acceptable?
    - Technology: Are there adequate numbers of back up devices for critical systems? Can third-party service providers assist in recovering lost or damaged data?

- User Response Activities
    - People: Can employees safely return to an operational state?
    - Process: Does the company need to control access to services to select individuals first (e.g., finance, logistics, etc.)

- Technology: Can technology resolve immediate problems from the recovery vice the employee such as, for example, reselecting printers and other data connections?

MORE COMPLETE ANSWER: In those situations, when control is specifically discussing a policy solution, the employment of automated tools, alerts, etc., should always be considered. Even the use of essential tracking tools such as Microsoft ® Excel ® and Access ® will at least demonstrate a level of positive control over the IT environment.

ASSESSMENT OBJECTIVE *Determine if:*		
SUB-CTRL	**DESCRIPTION**	**RECOMMENDED APPROACH**
3.6.1[a]	An operational incident-handling capability is established.	NCR
3.6.1[b]	The operational incident-handling capability includes preparation.	NCR
3.6.1[c]	The operational incident-handling capability includes detection.	NCR
3.6.1[d]	The operational incident-handling capability includes analysis.	NCR/PO/W-(It may be unreasonable for a small business to have any analytic capability other than a collection of logs and referral to the agency for action; a Waiver may be needed)
3.6.1[e]	The operational incident-handling capability includes containment.	NCR
3.6.1[f]	The operational incident-handling capability includes recovery.	NCR
3.6.1[g]	The operational incident-handling capability includes user response activities.	NCR

3.6.2 Track, document, and report incidents to appropriate officials and/or authorities both internal and external to the organization.

MINIMUM ANSWER: This control discusses the reporting requirements based on the severity of the incident as described above and within DOD's Precedence Categorization above. Ensure some form of the repository is maintained that an auditor could review at any time. Another reminder is that such information should be secured and encrypted at least at the CUI/CDI level.

MORE COMPLETE ANSWER: A complete response may include a dedicated computer server repository that could be physically disconnected from the system when not needed. This could prevent unauthorized access if an intruder is attempting to conduct intelligence collection or **reconnaissance** of the system; this would deny intruders' critical network information and add confusion for their penetration activities.

ASSESSMENT OBJECTIVE *Determine if:*		
SUB-CTRL	DESCRIPTION	RECOMMENDED APPROACH
3.6.2[a]	Incidents are tracked.	NCR
3.6.2[b]	Incidents are documented.	NCR
3.6.2[c]	Authorities to whom incidents are to be reported are identified.	NCR
3.6.2[d]	Organizational officials to whom incidents are to be reported are identified.	NCR
3.6.2[e]	Identified authorities are notified of incidents.	NCR
3.6.2[f]	Identified organizational officials are notified of incidents.	NCR

Derived Security Requirements:

3.6.3 Test the organizational incident response capability.
MINIMUM ANSWER: Test the IR Plan at least annually. This should include both internal and external notional penetration exercises. These may consist of

compromised login information and passwords provided to designated IT personnel. Ensure the results of the test are documented, reviewed, and signed by senior management. An IR test event should be maintained for any future audit. MORE COMPLETE ANSWER: This is not a requirement of this control and poses many risks to the IT environment. Do not recommend this solution; this would only be required based on the sensitivity of data, and the DOD directs penetration Testing (PENTEST). It is only offered for more of an appreciation of the complexity that a PENTEST entails.

A more expensive solution is hiring an outside Penetration Testing (PENTEST) company. Ensure that Rules of Engagement (ROE) are well established. Rules that should be affirmed by both the company and the PENTESTER, for example, is that no inadvertent change or destruction of data is authorized. The PENTEST company may also require a liability release for any unintentional damage caused by the PENTEST. Always coordinate with legal professionals experienced in such matters to avoid any damage or confusion created by unclear expectations of a PENTEST.

MAINTENANCE (MA)
How do you take care of IT?

The MA security control family is relatively easy to address concerning the requirements of NIST 800-171. This control requires processes and procedures that provide oversight of third-party vendors that offer IT maintenance and support. While this may appear vaguely paranoid, the company is required to exercise control of all maintenance personnel that potentially will have access to the company's and DOD's resident CUI/CDI and data. This will also typically require company escorts whose background has been appropriately checked and authorized to oversee outside workers.

Lack of maintenance or a failure to perform maintenance can result in the unauthorized disclosure of CUI/CDI. The full implementation of this requirement is contingent on the finalization of the proposed CUI/CDI federal regulation and marking guidance in the **CUI Registry**. (The marking requirements have been completed, and it is best to refer to the Registry, https://www.archives.gov/cui/registry/category-list, for specified industry codes.) These markings should be applied to business CUI/CDI data as well as IT hardware such as servers, desktops, laptops, etc.

Basic Security Requirements:

3.7.1 Perform maintenance on organizational information systems.
MINIMUM ANSWER: This should describe the company's maintenance procedures for its IT infrastructure. This could include either internal maintenance teams or third-party companies. This will consist of hardware component repairs and replacements, printer repairs, etc. Any maintenance agreements should be provided as artifacts to support an authorization package.

MORE COMPLETE ANSWER: Maintenance could include the identification of computer hardware spares on-site or at company warehouse locations. The company's logistics personnel should manage operational spares; they should be captured within the property book database and its associated hard copy reporting to senior management.

3.7.2 Provide effective controls on the tools, techniques, mechanisms, and personnel used to conduct information system maintenance.
MINIMUM ANSWER: This control relates to tools used for diagnostics and repairs of the company's IT system/network. These tools include, for example, hardware/software diagnostic test equipment and hardware/software **packet sniffers**. Access to the

hardware tools should be secured in lockable containers, and only accessed by authorized IT personnel.

In the case of software tools, they should be restricted to personnel with privileged user rights and specifically audited when any user is required or needed.

MORE COMPLETE ANSWER: Suggested additional control may include two-person integrity requirements. This would require that when any of these types of tools are utilized, there should be at least two authorized individuals involved in any system maintenance or diagnostic activities.

ASSESSMENT OBJECTIVE *Determine if:*		
SUB-CTRL	**DESCRIPTION**	**RECOMMENDED APPROACH**
3.7.2[a]	*Tools used to conduct system maintenance are controlled.*	NCR
3.7.2[b]	*Techniques used to conduct system maintenance are controlled.*	NCR
3.7.2[c]	*Mechanisms used to conduct system maintenance are controlled.*	NCR
3.7.2[d]	*Personnel used to conduct system maintenance are controlled.*	NCR

Derived Security Requirements:

3.7.3 Ensure equipment removed for off-site maintenance is sanitized of any CUI.

MINIMUM ANSWER: Company data should be backed-up locally and secured for a future reinstall on another storage device or the returned/repaired IT component. Also, the data should specifically be "wiped" by an industry-standard application for data deletion. Many software tools conduct multiple "passes" of data wipes to ensure the sanitization of the media.

MORE COMPLETE ANSWER: Any reports produced by the data "wiping" program could be captured in an equipment data log to provide proof of the action. Maintaining a hard copy of a soft copy spreadsheet or database log would be helpful. Future inspections by DOD may check this procedure to confirm the continuous application and repeatability of this procedure.

3.7.4 Check media containing diagnostic and test programs for malicious code before the media are used in the information system.

MINIMUM ANSWER: The ideal solution for this is to conduct a scan using corporate anti-virus software applications.

MORE COMPLETE ANSWER: A more thorough solution would include the use of an anti-malware application. Anti-malware programs are more comprehensive and proactively monitor **endpoints**, i.e., computers, laptops, servers, etc. (Anti-virus is not always designed to identify and clean malware, adware, worms, etc., from infected storage devices).

3.7.5 Require multifactor authentication to establish nonlocal maintenance sessions via external network connections and terminate such connections when nonlocal maintenance is complete.

MINIMUM ANSWER: Nonlocal maintenance is those diagnostic or repair activities conducted over network communications to include the Internet or dedicated least circuits.

This requires that any external third-party maintenance activities use some form of Multi-Factor Authentication (MFA) to access company IT hardware and software components directly. If IT personnel, working with outside maintainers can use an MFA solution, then the company most likely has a robust IT support capability. If not, then this control is a good candidate for an early POAM; ensure good milestones are established for monthly review, for example, "on-going research," "market survey of potential candidate solutions," "identification of funding sources," etc.

MORE COMPLETE ANSWER: A complete answer requires a technical solution. As discussed earlier, the use of CAC, PIV cards, or tokens, such as the RSA ®

RSA Token (R)

rotating encryption keying devices, are ideal solutions. This solution most likely will require additional analysis and funding approaches to select the most appropriate answer.

ASSESSMENT OBJECTIVE *Determine if:*		
SUB-CTRL	DESCRIPTION	RECOMMENDED APPROACH
3.7.5[a]	Multifactor authentication is used to establish nonlocal maintenance sessions via external network connections.	NCR
3.7.5[b]	Nonlocal maintenance sessions established via external network connections are terminated when nonlocal maintenance is complete.	NCR

3.7.6 Supervise the maintenance activities of maintenance personnel without required access authorization.

MINIMUM ANSWER: The procedure requirement should reflect that non-company maintenance personnel should always be escorted. An access log should be maintained, and it should include, for example, the individual or individuals, the represented company, the equipment repaired/diagnosed, the arrival and departure times, and the assigned escort. Maintain this hard-copy of soft-copy logs for future auditing purposes.

MORE COMPLETE ANSWER: Procedural enhancements could include confirmed background checks of third-party maintainers and picture identification compared with the on-site individual. These additional enhancements should be based upon the sensitivity of the company's data. Any unattended CUI/CDI data should always be secured by CUI/CDI procedures—in a lockable container.

MEDIA PROTECTION (MP)
Create, protect, and destroy

The MP control was written to handle the challenges of managing and protecting the computer media storing CUI/CDI. This would include DOD concerns about removable hard drives and especially the ability for a threat to employ the use of a Universal Serial Bus (USB) "thumb drive."

> **Special Topic: DOD USB Policy**
>
> A UNIVERSAL SERIAL BUS (USB) OR **THUMB DRIVE** WHILE PROVIDING GREAT FLEXIBILITY TO MOVE DATA TO AND FROM SYSTEM DATA STORES, THEY ARE ALSO MAJOR MEANS TO INJECT MALICIOUS SOFTWARE SUCH AS VIRUSES AND RANSOMWARE INTO A COMPANY'S SECURITY BOUNDARY. DOD PROHIBITS USB USE IN DOD ENVIRONMENTS. IT'S CRITICAL TO ADDRESS THE PROPER CARE AND USE OF THESE IN A COMPANY'S IT INFRASTRUCTURE AND ASSOCIATED PROCEDURE GUIDE.

While most computer users are aware of the convenience of the thumb drive to help store, transfer, and maintain data, it is also a well-known threat vector where criminals and foreign threats can introduce dangerous malware and viruses into unsuspecting users' computers. DOD forbids their use except under particular and controlled instances.

MP is also about assurances by the business that proper destruction and sanitization of old storage devices has occurred. There are many instances where DOD and other federal agencies have not implemented an effective sanitization process, and inadvertent disclosure of national security data has been released to the public. Cases include salvage companies discovering hard drives and dispose of computers containing CUI/CDI and, in many instances, national security classified information, has occurred.

Be especially mindful that the sanitization process requires high-grade industry or government-approved applications that entirely and effectively destroys all data on the target drive. Other procedures may include physical shredding of the drive or destruction methods that further prevent the reconstruction of any virtual data by unauthorized personnel.

Basic Security Requirements:

RISK MANAGEMENT'S FOUNDATION:

MITIGATE OR REDUCE,
NOT ELIMINATION
OF THE RISK OR THREAT

3.8.1 Protect (i.e., physically control and securely store) information system media containing CUI, both paper and digital.

MINIMUM ANSWER: To implement this control, the business should establish procedures regarding both CUI/CDI physical (paper) and virtual (disk drives) media. This should include only authorized personnel having access to individual and corporate sensitive data with necessary background checks and training. A business can use the foundations of other control families to mitigate further or reduce risks/threats.

A company can use other controls such as *more* training, longer audit log retention, *more* guards, or *more* complex passwords to **mitigate** any control. This would more clearly demonstrate to DOD that the firm has an actual implementation of these security controls.

The use of other mitigating controls within NIST 800-171 is specifically about **risk reduction.** Any effort to use other families of controls to meet a specific control improves the overall IT infrastructure's security posture and is highly recommended.

MORE COMPLETE ANSWER: The MP control can be further demonstrated by safeguarding physical files in secure or fire-resistant vaults. This could also include requirements for only IT personnel issuing property hand receipts for computer equipment or devices; a sound accountability system is essential.

ASSESSMENT OBJECTIVE *Determine if:*		
SUB-CTRL	*DESCRIPTION*	**RECOMMENDED APPROACH**
3.8.1[a]	*Paper media containing CUI is physically controlled.*	NCR

3.8.1[b]	Digital media containing CUI is physically controlled.	NCR
3.8.1[c]	Paper media containing CUI is securely stored.	NCR (Typically demonstrated by securing within a lockable container, desk, etc., and the individual/s authorized access are the only ones identified to enter, remove, or destroy CUI data from its holding area.)
3.8.1[d]	Digital media containing CUI is securely stored.	NCR

3.8.2 Limit access to CUI on information system media to authorized users.
MINIMUM ANSWER: Identify in policy documents which, by name, title, or function, has access to specified CUI/CDI. Any artifacts should include the policy document and an associated by-name roster of personnel assigned access by-system, e.g., accounting system, ordering system, patent repository, medical records, etc.

MORE COMPLETE ANSWER: A complete response could include logging of authorized personnel and providing a print-out of accesses over one month.

3.8.3 Sanitize or destroy information system media containing CUI before disposal or release for reuse.
MINIMUM ANSWER: A good policy description is a must regarding data destruction of sensitive information within DOD. Either use a commercial-grade "wiping" program or physically destroy the drive.

If the company is either planning to internally reuse or sell to outside repurposing companies, ensure that the wiping is a commercial grade or approved by DOD. There are companies providing disk shredding or destruction services. Provide any service agreements that should specify the type and level of data destruction to DOD assessors.

MORE COMPLETE ANSWER: For any DOD assessment, the media sanitization company should provide **destruction certificates**. Chose several selected destruction certificates to include in the DOD BOE submission. Typically, logistics and supply ordering sections of the business should manage as part of the Supply Chain Risk Management (SCRM) process.

ASSESSMENT OBJECTIVE *Determine if:*		
SUB-CTRL	*DESCRIPTION*	**RECOMMENDED APPROACH**
3.8.3[a]	*System media containing CUI is sanitized or destroyed before disposal.*	NCR
3.8.3[b]	*System media containing CUI is sanitized before it is released for reuse.*	NCR

A SIDE DISCUSSION ON SUPPLY CHAIN RISK MANAGEMENT

SCRM is a relatively new concern within the federal government. It is part of securing IT products within the business.

Questions that should be considered include:

- Is this product produced by the US or by an Ally?
- Could counterfeit IT items be purchased from less-than-reputable entities?
- Is this IT product from an approved hardware/software product listing?

Users innately trust software developers to provide security updates for their software applications and products that would add new functionalities or fix security vulnerabilities. They would not expect updates to be infected with malicious scripts, codes, or programming. Most users have no mechanisms (or no concerns) about defending against seemingly legitimate software that is duly signed. Unfortunately, software unwittingly accessed by users and tainted by either nation-state actors or general cyber-criminals on the Internet poses an alarming risk to the global IT supply chain.

The use of varied supply chain attacks by cyber attackers to access corporate software development infrastructures has been major vectors of concerns for the government as well as the private sector. These attacks typically include targeting publicly connected software build, test, update servers, and other portions of a software company's software development environment. Nation-state agents can then inject malware into software updates, and releases have far-ranging impacts on the IT supply chain; the challenge continues to grow.[14]

Users become infected through official software distribution channels that are trusted. Attackers can add their malware to the development infrastructure of software vendors before they are compiled[15]; hence, the malware is signed with the digital identity of a legitimate software vendor. This exploit bypasses typical "whitelisting" security measures making it difficult to identify the intrusion. This has contributed to a high degree of success by malicious cyber threat actors. Some example recent intrusions include:

---

[14] Other less-protected portions of the supply chain include, for example, Field Programmable Gate Arrays (FPGA) and Application-Specific Integrated Circuit (ASIC) chips found on most major US weapons and satellite systems.

[15] Before they are converted as an executable (.exe) that are injected at the programming level where quality control mechanisms are often less-than adequate in secure development processes

- In July 2017, Chinese cyber espionage operatives changed the software packages of a legitimate software vendor, NetSarang Computer (https://www.netsarang.com/). These changes allowed access to a broad range of industries and institutions that included retail locations, financial services, transportation, telecommunications, energy, media, and academics.

- In August 2017, hackers inserted a backdoor into updates of the computer "cleanup" program, **CCleaner**, while it was in its software development phases.

- In June 2017, suspected Russian actors **deployed the** PETYA ransomware to a wide-range of European targets by compromising a targeted Ukrainian software vendor

Supply chain compromises have been ongoing for years. However, they have been remote and covert[16]. They may follow with follow-on intrusions of targets later and provide a means for general hacking and damage to the company targets. The use of such compromises offers likely means for support nation-state cyber espionage, including those identified from Chinese IT equipment product producers and manufacturers. These include such companies, such as Chinese-based companies to include ZTE, Lenovo, and Huawei.

This trend continues to grow as there are more points in the supply chain that the attackers can penetrate using advanced techniques. The techniques involved have become publicly discussed enough, and their proven usefulness encourages others to use these vectors of attack specific to damage and reconnaissance of governments, businesses, and agencies globally. Advanced actors will likely continue to leverage this activity to conduct cyber espionage, cybercrime, and disruption. The dangers to the supply chain are of growing concern as the threat and risk landscapes continue to increase for the foreseeable future.

For further information, see NIST 800-161, *Supply Chain Risk Management Practices for Federal Information Systems and Organizations.* (http://nvlpubs.nist.gov/nistpubs/SpecialPublications/NIST.SP.800-161.pdf).

---

[16] Disclosing such information by a business may have both legal and reputation impacts; current US law under the 2015 Computer Information Security Act (CISA) does allow for "safe harbor" protections in the US.

ALSO SEE THE AUTHOR'S RECENT BOOK ON THIS TOPIC:

A GUIDE FOR SUPPLY CHAIN RISK MANAGEMENT (SCRM) APPLICATION IN THE REAL WORLD. Welcome to the next iteration of SCRM. From the internationally acclaimed cybersecurity thought-leader, Mr. Russo provides two distinct NIST 800-161, "Supply Chain Risk Management Practices for Federal Information Systems and Organizations," approaches to resolve the modern-day challenge of SCRM. The solutions, while similar, provide a 21st Century resolution to a better approach in a systematic way to prevent compromises to the US and global IT supply chain. The use of varied supply chain attacks by cyber attackers to access, for example, software development infrastructures, have been significant vectors of concerns for governments as well as the private sector. These attacks typically include targeting publicly connected software "build, test, update servers," and other portions of a software development environment. Nation-state agents can then inject malware into software updates, and subsequent releases have far-ranging impacts on the IT supply chain; the challenge continues to grow. SCRM 1.0 is a concept for establishing an effective and repeatable process that can be applied against standard supply chain components such as hardware, firmware, software, etc. The author introduces SCRM 2.0, much like SCRM 1.0 (Product-based approach); the need is to turn to a much more precarious aspect of SCRM. We must consider the service piece of SCRM that includes the people, companies, and organizations along the supply chain that may also be compromised within the global marketing of IT equipment and capabilities. This is the next most significant issue facing the field of cybersecurity protection in the 21st Century.

Derived Security Requirements:

3.8.4 Mark media with necessary CUI markings and distribution limitations. MINIMUM ANSWER: This includes the marking of both physical documents as well as soft-copy versions. The best way to answer this is by referencing the following National Archives and Record Administration (NARA) document as part of the company's procedural guide that addresses this control:

- *See Chapter on CUI Marking and Handling.*
- *Marking Controlled Unclassified Information*, Version 1.1 – December 6, 2016. (https://www.archives.gov/files/cui/20161206-cui-marking-handbook-v1-1.pdf)

EXAMPLE PROCEDURE: "All company personnel will mark CUI/CDI, physical and virtual data, per the National Archives and Record Administration (NARA), Marking Controlled Unclassified Information, Version 1.1 – December 6, 2016. If there are questions about marking requirements, employees will refer these questions to their immediate supervisor or the corporate CUI/CDI officer."

MORE COMPLETE ANSWER: This could include a screen capture that shows a DOD representative that onscreen access to CUI/CDI data is appropriately marked. A firm could also assign a CUI/CDI marking specialist; this person should be an individual with prior security experience and familiar with DOD marking requirements. For example, this individual could additionally provide quarterly "brown bag" sessions where the "CUI/CDI Security Officer" provides training during lunchtime sessions. Be creative when considering more thorough means to reinforce cybersecurity control requirements.

ASSESSMENT OBJECTIVE Determine if:		
SUB-CTRL	DESCRIPTION	RECOMMENDED APPROACH
3.8.4[a]	Media containing CUI is marked with applicable CUI markings.	NCR
3.8.4[b]	Media containing CUI is marked with distribution limitations.	NCR

3.8.5 Control access to media containing CUI and maintain accountability for media during transport outside of controlled areas.

MINIMUM ANSWER: This control is about "transport outside of controlled areas." This, too, is a matter of only authorized individuals (couriers) be authorized by position, training, and security checks that should be considered when the company needs to transport CUI/CDI external to its typical corporate location.

Individuals should be provided either courier cards or orders that are signed by an authorized company representative typically responsible for oversight of security matters. This could be, for example, the corporate security officer, Information System Security Manager (ISSM), or their designated representative. These individuals should be readily known to other employees and managers who have demanded to move CUI/CDI to outside locations. This would demonstrate that there are available and on-call personnel based on the business mission and priorities. This also should be a limited cadre of staff that management relies on for such external courier services.

MORE COMPLETE ANSWER: The company could hire an outside contract service that transports both physical and computer media containing CUI/CDI based on the company's mission.

ASSESSMENT OBJECTIVE Determine if:		
SUB-CTRL	DESCRIPTION	RECOMMENDED APPROACH
3.8.5[a]	Access to media containing CUI is controlled.	NCR

| 3.8.5[b] | Accountability for media containing CUI is maintained during transport outside of controlled areas. | NCR |

3.8.6 Implement cryptographic mechanisms to protect the confidentiality of CUI stored on digital media during transport unless otherwise protected by alternative physical safeguards.

MINIMUM ANSWER: This is a Data at Rest (DAR) issue. See Control 3.1.3 for depiction. The recommendation is that all CUI/CDI need to be encrypted. A typical application that has been used by DOD is BitLocker ®. It provides password protection to "lockdown" any transportable media. It is not the only solution, and many solutions can be used to secure DAR.

The 256-bit key length is the common standard for commercial and DOD encryption applications for hard drives, removable drives, and even USB devices. DOD requires DAR must always be encrypted; it is best to resource and research acceptable tools that DOD supports and recognizes.

MORE COMPLETE ANSWER: The reinforcing of this control may include using enhanced physical security measures. This could consist of hardened and lockable carry cases. Only authorized employees should transport designated CUI/CDI. This should also be captured in the submitted BOE to DOD.

3.8.7 Control the use of removable media on information system components.
MINIMUM ANSWER: Identify in corporate policy the types and kinds of removable media that can be attached to fixed desktop and laptop computers. These could include external hard drives, optical drives, or USB thumb drives.

Strongly recommend that thumb drives are not used; if needed, then designate IT security personnel who can authorize their restricted use. This should also include anti-virus/malware scans before their use.

MORE COMPLETE ANSWER: Removeable media drives can be "blocked" by changes in system **registry** settings; company IT personnel should be able to prevent such designated devices from accessing the computer and accessing the company network.

3.8.8 Prohibit the use of portable storage devices when such devices have no identifiable owner.
MINIMUM ANSWER: This should be established in the company procedure. If such devices are found, they should be surrendered to security and scanned immediately for any viruses, malware, etc.

MORE COMPLETE ANSWER: As described in Control 3.8.7, IT personnel can block unauthorized devices from attaching to the computer/network by updating registry settings.

3.8.9 Protect the confidentiality of backup CUI at storage locations.
MINIMUM ANSWER: *This is a Data at Rest (DAR) issue.* See Control 3.1.3 for a depiction. See Control 3.8.6 for suggested requirements for the protection of CUI/CDI under a DAR solution.

MORE COMPLETE ANSWER: See Control 3.8.6 for additional means to protect CUI/CDI.

PERSONNEL SECURITY (PS)
Background Checks

This is a relatively simple control. It most likely is already implemented within the company and only requires procedural documents are provided in the submission to DOD. This should include both civil and criminal background checks using a reputable company that can process the individual background checks through the Federal Bureau of Investigation (FBI). Background Checking companies can also do other forms of personnel checks to include personal social media presence or financial solvency matters that may avoid any future embarrassment for the company.

While these checks are not well defined for the company's under NIST 800-171, it should meet minimum government standards for a **Public Trust** review. Discuss with the Contract Officer what the requirements they suggest be achieved to provide the level of background check required to meet the NIST 800-171 requirement. Also, it is always best to work with HR and legal experts when formulating a personnel security policy to include the types and kinds of investigations are following applicable state and federal law in this area.

Basic Security Requirements:

3.9.1 Screen individuals prior to authorizing access to information systems containing CUI.

MINIMUM ANSWER: This control requires some form of background check to be conducted for employees. Several firms can provide criminal and civil background checks based upon an individual's personal information and their fingerprints.

The company should capture its HR process regarding background checks in the company cybersecurity procedure document. It is also essential to address when a reinvestigation is required. The suggestion is at least every three years or upon recognition by managers of potential legal occurrences that may include financial problems, domestic violence, etc. This control should be highly integrated with the company's HR and legal policies.

MORE COMPLETE ANSWER: Some background companies can, for an additional fee, conduct active monitoring of individuals when significant personal or financial changes occur in a person's life — update company procedural guides with all details of the company's established process.

3.9.2 Ensure that CUI and information systems containing CUI are protected during and after personnel actions such as terminations and transfers.
MINIMUM ANSWER: This control is about procedures regarding whether termination is amicable or not. Always have clear terms about non-removal of corporate data and CUI/CDI after departure from the company to include databases, customer listings, and proprietary data/IP. This should consist of legal implications for violation of the policy.

MORE COMPLETE ANSWER: The technical solution could include monitoring by IT staff of all account activity during the out-processing period. This could also include immediate account lock-outs on the departure date. Also recommend that there are changes to all vault combinations, building accesses, etc., that the individual had specific access to during their tenure.

ASSESSMENT OBJECTIVE *Determine if:*		
SUB-CTRL	*DESCRIPTION*	**RECOMMENDED APPROACH**
3.9.2[a]	*A policy and/or process for terminating system access and any credentials coincident with personnel actions is established.*	NCR
3.9.2[b]	*System access and credentials are terminated consistent with personnel actions such as termination or transfer.*	NCR
3.9.2[c]	*The system is protected during and after personnel transfer actions.*	P- An update should include changes or updates in accesses when an employee transfers to another location or office.

Derived Security Requirements: None.

PHYSICAL PROTECTION (PP)
Guards and moats

Physical security is part of a company's overall protection of its people and facilities. A little-known fact is that the guiding principle for any *true* cybersecurity professional is to protect the life and safety of the people supported. This control is also about the protection of damage to corporate assets, facilities, or equipment; this includes any loss or destruction of the material computer equipment secured by the PP security control. This controls addresses the physical security that also includes such elements as guards, alarm systems, cameras, etc., that help the company protect its sensitive company data and, of course, its NIST 800-171 CUI.

There are no limits on how to harden a company's "castle walls," but for any owner, the cost is always a significant consideration. Protecting vital CUI/CDI while seemingly expansive under this control allows for reasonable flexibility. Again, the company should reasonably define its success under the NIST 800-171 controls. "Success" can be distinguished from the company's point of view regarding complexity or cost but must be prepared to defend any proposed solution to DOD assessors.

Basic Security Requirements:

3.10.1 Limit physical access to organizational information systems, equipment, and the respective operating environments to authorized individuals.

MINIMUM ANSWER: Of importance for this control is limiting access to corporate data servers, backup devices, and specifically, the "computer farm." If the company is maintaining devices on its premises, then policy should address who has authorized access to such sensitive areas.

If the corporation is using an off-site **Cloud Service Provider (CSP)**, capture in part or full sections of any CSP service agreements such as a Cloud Service Level Agreement (CSLA), this should include any specific actions and control measures for any physical security protection.

Both types of computer architectures, on-premise, and cloud should address. For example, such areas of interest to include access logs, after-hours access, camera monitoring, unauthorized access reporting criteria, types, and kinds of network defense devices such as Intrusion Detection and Prevention Systems (IDS/IPS), etc., as part of the corporate procedure.

MORE COMPLETE ANSWER: This could include active alerting to both management and security personnel that includes phone calls, email alerts, or SMS text messages to designated company security personnel. Security measures and **alert thresholds** should be driven by the sensitivity of the data stored. Management should make **risk-based** determinations of the cost and returns on effectiveness to drive the corporate policy for this control as well as other solutions.

ASSESSMENT OBJECTIVE *Determine if:*		
SUB-CTRL	*DESCRIPTION*	**RECOMMENDED APPROACH**
3.10.1[a]	Authorized individuals allowed physical access are identified.	NCR
3.10.1[b]	Physical access to organizational systems is limited to authorized individuals.	NCR
3.10.1[c]	Physical access to equipment is limited to authorized individuals.	NCR
3.10.1[d]	Physical access to operating environments is limited to authorized individuals.	NCR

3.10.2 Protect and monitor the physical facility and support infrastructure for those information systems.

MINIMUM/MORE COMPLETE ANSWER: This control can be addressed in many ways by physical security measures. This should include locked doors, cipher locks, safes, security cameras, guard forces, etc. This control should be answered by the current physical protections that prevent direct entry into the company and physical access to its IT devices and networks.

ASSESSMENT OBJECTIVE		
Determine if:		
SUB-CTRL	***DESCRIPTION***	**RECOMMENDED APPROACH**
3.10.2[a]	*The physical facility where organizational systems reside is protected.*	NCR
3.10.2[b]	*The support infrastructure for organizational systems is protected.*	NCR- (This would include all physical barriers to entries into computer spaces, server rooms, etc., for unauthorized personnel)
3.10.2[c]	*The physical facility where organizational systems reside is monitored.*	NCR -(typically, cameras or guards)
3.10.2[d]	*The support infrastructure for organizational systems is monitored.*	NCR

Derived Security Requirements:

3.10.3 Escort visitors and monitor visitor activity.

MINIMUM ANSWER: Much as described under the MA control above, like security measures as described in Control 3.7.6, should be employed.

MORE COMPLETE ANSWER: Also, refer to Control 3.7.6 on more significant security measures that can be used to demonstrate complete compliance with this control.

ASSESSMENT OBJECTIVE		
Determine if:		
SUB-CTRL	***DESCRIPTION***	**RECOMMENDED APPROACH**
3.10.3[a]	*Visitors are escorted.*	NCR

| 3.10.3[b] | Visitor activity is monitored. | NCR – (Escorts, guards, and cameras inclusive) |

3.10.4 Maintain audit logs of physical access.

MINIMUM/MORE COMPLETE ANSWER: Refer to Control 3.7.6 for suggested audit log items. This should address personnel during operating and after-hour entry into the company and its IT facilities. This should include logs specific to outside third-party vendors and subcontractors; any such procedures should also apply to those individuals who are not direct employees.

3.10.5 Control and manage physical access devices.

MINIMUM ANSWER: This control requires that physical access devices such as security badges, combinations, and physical keys are managed through both procedures and logs (physical or automated). The company needs to demonstrate to the government its positive security measures to protect its CUI/CDI data. While this control may appear easier than the technical policy control settings used by the company for its IT systems, it is no less critical.

MORE COMPLETE ANSWER: If not already in place, identify and separate the physical security functions (e.g., facility security officer, etc.) from the technical security functions managed by corporate IT personnel with the requisite skills and experiences. Companies should avoid duty-creep on its cybersecurity personnel and define roles and responsibilities between its classic security functions (e.g., physical, personnel security, etc.) and the roles and responsibilities of its cyber workforce that may reduce their effectiveness of both security areas.

ASSESSMENT OBJECTIVE Determine if:		
SUB-CTRL	DESCRIPTION	RECOMMENDED APPROACH
3.10.5[a]	Physical access devices are identified.	NCR
3.10.5[b]	Physical access devices are controlled.	NCR

3.10.5[c]	Physical access devices are managed.	NCR

Cybersecurity workforce duty-creep is a real-world occurrence; Companies are unwittingly shifting overall "security" functions from classic security personnel to cybersecurity professionals creating overall security gaps for a company or agency

3.10.6 Enforce safeguarding measures for CUI at alternate worksites (e.g., telework sites).

MINIMUM ANSWER: (See Control 3.1.3 for the explanation of DAR and DIT). DAR application solutions can quickly address this control. Laptops should always be password protected; this should be part of any central cybersecurity policy document and enforced by technical solutions deployed by company IT personnel. Additionally, The DIT protections are afforded by corporate VPN and 2FA/MFA solutions.

MORE COMPLETE ANSWER: The company should establish minimum requirements for telework protection. This could include, for example, work should be conducted in a physically securable area, the VPN should always be used, corporate assets should not use unsecured networks such as at coffee shops, fast-food restaurants, etc. This could also include an explicit telework agreement for employees before being authorized telework permission, and it should be carefully coordinated with HR and legal experts.

ASSESSMENT OBJECTIVE		
Determine if:		
SUB-CTRL	*DESCRIPTION*	**RECOMMENDED APPROACH**
3.10.6[a]	*Safeguarding measures for CUI are defined for alternate work sites.*	NCR
3.10.6[b]	*Safeguarding measures for CUI are enforced for alternate work sites.*	NCR

RISK ASSESSMENT (RA)
Dealing with Changes to the Infrastructure

The RA control relies on a continual process to determine whether changes in hardware, software or architecture create either a significant positive or negative **security-relevant** effect. This is typically done by using a **Change Request** (CR). If an upgrade to, for example, the Windows 10 ® Secure Host Baseline Operating System software, and it improves the security posture of the network, a Risk Assessment (RA) is needed, and associated **risk analysis** should be performed by authorized technical personnel. This could take the form of a technical report that management accepts from its IT staff for approval or disapproval of the change. Management, working with its IT staff, should determine thresholds when a formal RA activity needs to occur.

The RA process affords a significant amount of flexibility during the life of the system and should be used when other-than, for example, a new application or **security patches** are applied. Security patches updates are typically integrated into Operating Systems and applications. IT personnel should also regularly manually check for typical functional patches and security patch updates from the software companies' websites.

"Negative" security-relevant effects on the corporate IT infrastructure include, for example, a major re-architecture event or a move to a Cloud Service Provider. While these events may not seem "negative," NIST and DOD standards require a full reassessment. In other words, plan accordingly if the company is going to embark on a significant overhaul of its IT system. There will be a need under these circumstances to consider the impacts on the company's current Authority to Operate (ATO). These types of events typically necessitate that the NIST 800-171 process is redone; prior work in terms of policies and procedures can be reused to receive an updated ATO.

The decision-tree below is designed to help a company determine when to consider an RA:

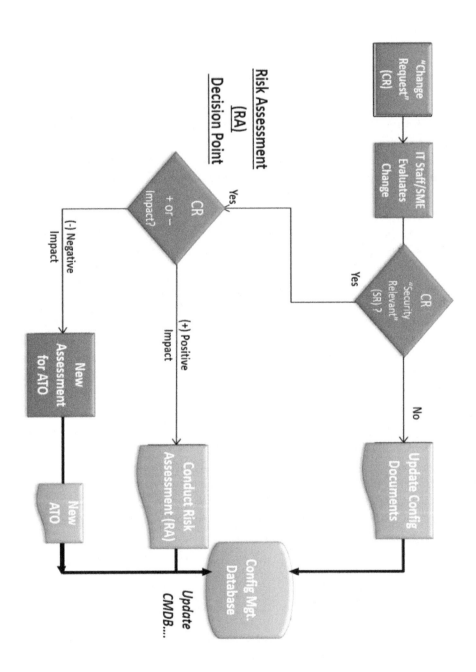

Decision-tree Addressing "Security Relevance"

Basic Security Requirements:

3.11.1 Periodically assess the risk to organizational operations (including mission, functions, image, or reputation), organizational assets, and individuals, resulting from the operation of organizational information systems and the associated processing, storage, or transmission of CUI.

MINIMUM ANSWER: RA's are required when there is a "major" change due to either a hardware change (e.g., replacing an old firewall with a new Cisco ® firewall), software version upgrades (e.g., moving from Adobe ® 8.0 to 9.0), or changes to architecture (e.g., adding a new backup drive). The consideration is always about *how* this change to the baseline configuration is either a positive (normal) or negative (preferably, highly unlikely)?

It is crucial to describe the corporate RA process in terms of change needed and overall risk to the IT system. This should include who conducts the technical portion of the RA and who, in senior management, for example, the Chief Operating Officer (COO) or Chief Information Officer (CIO) that determines final approval.

This is as new to DOD Contracting as it is to the company; understand there will be "growing pains," as DOD continues to define its procedures.

While not thoroughly discussed as part of this book, **the integration of the NIST 800-171 with DOD contracting is in its infancy**. It is best to coordinate and advise DOD Contract Officers of the changes. It is always "best practice" to maintain a history of RA development and approval for future DOD auditing.

MORE COMPLETE ANSWER: Implementing a more defined RA process could include standardized formats for RA artifacts. This could consist of a technical report written by knowledgeable IT personnel about a change, or a simplified form that allows for a checklist-like approach. It could also employ an outside third-party company that would formalize a review of the changes and their analysis of the overall impact on system security.

ASSESSMENT OBJECTIVE *Determine if:*		
SUB-CTRL	DESCRIPTION	RECOMMENDED APPROACH
3.11.1[a]	The frequency to assess risk to organizational operations, organizational assets, and individuals is defined.	NCR – (See discussion above regarding RA's conducted annually)
3.11.1[b]	Risk to organizational operations, organizational assets, and individuals resulting from the operation of an organizational system that processes, stores, or transmits CUI is assessed with the defined frequency.	NCR

Derived Security Requirements:

3.11.2 Scan for vulnerabilities in the information system and applications periodically and when new vulnerabilities affecting the system are identified.

MINIMUM ANSWER: This control requires that the company (system owner) regularly scans for vulnerabilities in the information system and hosted applications based upon a defined frequency or randomly based upon an established policy or procedure. This is also supposed to be applied when new vulnerabilities affecting the system or applications are identified.

> **Reminder**
>
> **Supply Chain Risk Management (SCRM)**
>
> The Russian-based software developer, Kaspersky Lab's ® Anti-virus solutions are currently prohibited by the DOD.

The simplest way to address this control is by using **anti-virus** and **anti-malware** enterprise-levels of software versions. Major players in these areas include Symantec ®, McAfee ®, and Malwarebytes ®. Procedural documents should describe the products used to address "new vulnerabilities" using these solutions. See also SYSTEM AND INFORMATION INTEGRITY (SI) as a reinforcing control for this RA control.

MORE COMPLETE ANSWER: A suggested complete implementation could be the leveraging of company ISP services also is identified for providing a secondary layer of defense as a form of "trusted" connection. This could include any available SLA's that define the service provider's ability to mitigate such additional threats by employing **whitelisting** and **blacklisting** services; these services are designed to allow or restrict access depending on an **Access Control List** (ACL). See Control 3.14.2 for a more detailed description.

ASSESSMENT OBJECTIVE Determine if:		
SUB-CTRL	DESCRIPTION	RECOMMENDED APPROACH
3.11.2[a]	The frequency to scan for vulnerabilities in organizational systems and applications is defined.	NCR
3.11.2[b]	Vulnerability scans are performed on organizational systems with the defined frequency.	NCR
3.11.2[c]	Vulnerability scans are performed on applications with the defined frequency.	NCR – (typically monthly, but more often for major virus releases or "zero-day" threats)

3.11.2[d]	Vulnerability scans are performed on organizational systems when new vulnerabilities are identified.	NCR
3.11.2[e]	Vulnerability scans are performed on applications when new vulnerabilities are identified.	NCR

3.11.3 Remediate vulnerabilities in accordance with assessments of risk.

MINIMUM ANSWER: Typically, anti-virus and anti-malware security applications cannot only detect but remove and quarantine malicious software. Update documentation accordingly.

This control also addresses "vulnerabilities" that are created by not meeting a specific control within the identified NIST 800-171 families. To discuss these re-assessment activities, it is reasonable to update system POAM documentation with exact reasons any control is not met in full. This should attempt to answer what mitigation solutions are employed? When, by a specific date, the vulnerability will be corrected?

MORE COMPLETE ANSWER: Some additional means to better address this RA control is through other external services that can support ongoing remediation efforts. This could include the company's ISP or Cloud Service Providers. This could also include regular reviews of POAMs by both management and IT support staff personnel, for example, monthly or quarterly.

ASSESSMENT OBJECTIVE Determine if:		
SUB-CTRL	DESCRIPTION	RECOMMENDED APPROACH
3.11.3[a]	Vulnerabilities are identified.	NCR
3.11.3[b]	Vulnerabilities are remediated in accordance with risk assessments.	NCR

SECURITY ASSESSMENT (SA)
Beginning Continuous Monitoring and Control Reviews

    The SA control is about a process that re-assesses the state of all security controls and whether changes have occurred requiring additional mitigations of new risks or threats. Within DOD, the standard is 1/3rd of the controls are to be re-assessed annually. This would require designated IT personnel to conduct an SA event of approximately 36-37 controls per year. This should be captured in what is called a **ConMon Plan**. (See Appendix C, **CONTINUOUS MONITORING: A More Detailed Discussion** is an in-depth discussion of the current and future state of Continuous Monitoring and what it may mean to businesses).

    Continuous Monitoring is a vital component of the NIST 800 series cybersecurity protection framework. It is defined as "…maintaining ongoing awareness of information security, vulnerabilities, and threats to support organizational risk management decisions,"

(NIST Special Publication 800-137, *Information Security Continuous Monitoring (ISCM) for Federal Information Systems and Organizations*, http://nvlpubs.nist.gov/nistpubs/Legacy/SP/nistspecialpublication800-137.pdf).

ConMon is a significant guiding principle for the recurring execution of a Security Assessment

---

Basic Security Requirements:

3.12.1 Periodically assess the security controls in organizational information systems to determine if the controls are effective in their application.

MINIMUM ANSWER: As described in the opening paragraph, meeting the basic requirements of the Security Assessment control should include the creation of a ConMon Plan and a review of 33% of the controls at least annually.

MORE COMPLETE ANSWER: A more thorough execution could include more than 33%

of the controls being reviewed and reassessed; it is suggested to provide the results of annual Security Assessments to DOD contracting or their designated recipients.

ASSESSMENT OBJECTIVE *Determine if:*		
SUB-CTRL	*DESCRIPTION*	**RECOMMENDED APPROACH**
3.12.1[a]	*The frequency of security control assessments is defined.*	P- 1/3 of the controls should be assessed annually (typical)
3.12.1[b]	*Security controls are assessed with the defined frequency to determine if the controls are effective in their application.*	P-ConMon Plan will identify "...Security controls ... assessed with ... defined frequency to determine if the controls are effective in their application."

3.12.2 Develop and implement plans of action designed to correct deficiencies and reduce or eliminate vulnerabilities in organizational information systems. MINIMUM ANSWER: Where the company does not fully implement the security control or not recognized by DOD as being fully compliant, a detailed POAM is necessary; review guidance under the AC control for a more detailed discussion of what is required in preparing a POAM for review. (See the Introduction about major requirements for completing a POAM).

As described earlier, this should include activities that are meant to answer the control in full or at least leverage other physical and virtual elements of additional security controls to reinforce the posture of the control in question. A well-written POAM that is tracked and managed serves as the foundation for a robust risk management process.

> ***Cybersecurity is a leadership, not a technical challenge***

MORE COMPLETE ANSWER: Regular reviews by management and IT staff should enhance the company's cybersecurity posture. Cybersecurity is not just something that IT security personnel do; it includes the active oversight and review by corporate leadership to ensure effectiveness.

ASSESSMENT OBJECTIVE *Determine if:*		
SUB-CTRL	**DESCRIPTION**	**RECOMMENDED APPROACH**
3.12.2[a]	*Deficiencies and vulnerabilities to be addressed by the plan of action are identified.*	NCR – (The POAM)
3.12.2[b]	*A plan of action is developed to correct identified deficiencies and reduce or eliminate identified vulnerabilities.*	NCR
3.12.2[c]	*The plan of action is implemented to correct identified deficiencies and reduce or eliminate identified vulnerabilities.*	NCR

3.12.3 Monitor information system security controls on an ongoing basis to ensure the continued effectiveness of the controls.

MINIMUM ANSWER: This control can be answered in terms of a well-developed and executed ConMon Plan. Describing its purpose and the actions of assigned personnel to accomplish this task will answer this control.

MORE COMPLETE ANSWER: Suggested additional efforts regarding this control could include ad hoc spot checks of controls outside of the annual review process. Identify using the **PPT Model** described in Control 3.6.1, who is responsible for conducting the assessment (people), the workflow to adequately assess the current state of the control (process), and any supporting automation that provides feedback and reporting to management (technology).

3.12.4 Develop, document, and periodically update system security plans that describe system boundaries, system environments of operation, how security requirements are implemented, and the relationships with or connections to other systems.

MINIMUM ANSWER: this control requires that the **SSP** is updated regularly. The SSP should, at a minimum, be reviewed *annually* by designated company cybersecurity/IT personnel to ensure its accuracy. The SSP should be accurately updated sooner if there are significant changes to the:

- Hardware
- Software
- Network Architecture/Topology

MORE COMPLETE ANSWER: A more complete means to address this control is by addressing company change control boards. These are regular meetings when changes to hardware, software, or architecture occur. This should include mechanisms to document the occurrence of application and security patching. An effective procedure should always address changes to the IT system.

ASSESSMENT OBJECTIVE *Determine if:*		
SUB-CTRL	*DESCRIPTION*	**RECOMMENDED APPROACH**
3.12.4[a]	*A system security plan is developed.*	NCR – (The SSP)
3.12.4[b]	*The system boundary is described and documented in the system security plan.*	NCR (SSP)
3.12.4[c]	*The system environment of operation is described and documented in the system security plan.*	NCR (SSP)
3.12.4[d]	*The security requirements identified and approved by the designated authority as non-applicable are identified.*	NCR (SSP)

3.12.4[e]	The method of security requirement implementation is described and documented in the system security plan.	NCR (SSP)
3.12.4[f]	The relationship with or connection to other systems is described and documented in the system security plan.	NCR (SSP) – This is specific to external systems such as telecommunications carriers or other servers (computers) accessed by the local IT environment to meet its mission requirements
3.12.4[g]	The frequency to update the system security plan is defined.	P-The SSP should be updated when significant or more accurately, "security-relevant" changes happen to the IT environment.
3.12.4[h]	System security plan is updated with the defined frequency.	P-While changes to the SSP should be connected with significant changes for this sub-control we recommend an update at least every 90-180 days depending on the business or agencies complexity

Derived Security Requirements: None.

SYSTEM AND COMMUNICATIONS PROTECTION (SC)
External Communication and Connection Security

The overall risk management strategy is vital in establishing the appropriate technical solutions as well as procedural direction and guidance for the company. The core of this security control is that it creates policy based upon applicable federal laws, Executive Orders, directives, regulations, policies, standards, and guidance. This control focuses on information security policy that can reflect the complexity of a business and its operation with the DOD. The procedures should be established for the security of the overall IT architecture and specifically for the components (hardware and software) of the information system.

In this control, many of the prior reinforcing controls can be used in demonstrating to DOD a fuller understanding of NIST 800-171 requirements. The apparent repetition of other already developed technical solutions and procedural guides can be used as supporting these controls. However, corporate procedures must be addressed individually—this is for traceability purposes of any potential current or future audit of the company's work by DOD; clear and aligned explanations of the controls will make the approval process quicker.

Basic Security Requirements:

3.13.1 Monitor, control, and protect organizational communications (i.e., information transmitted or received by organizational information systems) at the external boundaries and key internal boundaries of the information systems.

MINIMUM ANSWER: This control can be answered in the corporate procedure and include, for example, active auditing that checks for unauthorized access, individuals (external) who have had numerous failed logins, and traffic entering the network from "blacklisted" addresses, etc. The company should refer to its specific audit procedure as described in more detail under the AU control.

MORE COMPLETE ANSWER: This control could be better met as formerly discussed by using "smart" firewalls and advanced SIEM solutions. While costlier and requiring more considerable technical experience, corporate leadership should consider it. These solutions, while not necessarily cost-effective for the current state of the company, it should be regarded as part of any future architectural change effort. Any planning efforts should consider current and future technology purchases meant to enhance the cybersecurity posture of the company. See Appendix C for a broader description of SIEM technologies and how they may become part of the IT infrastructure.

ASSESSMENT OBJECTIVE *Determine if:*		
SUB-CTRL	*DESCRIPTION*	**RECOMMENDED APPROACH**
3.13.1[a]	*The external system boundary is defined.*	P/SSP-The "external system" boundary here is specific to firewalls and DMZ's. **This is part of the SSP.** This control also addresses protections, and this is only meant to identify where the "security boundary" is defined and known.
3.13.1[b]	*Key internal system boundaries are defined.*	SSP
3.13.1[c]	*Communications are monitored at the external system boundary.*	P- "Communications are monitored at the external system boundary."
3.13.1[d]	*Communications are monitored at key internal boundaries.*	P- "Communications are monitored at key internal boundaries."
3.13.1[e]	*Communications are controlled at the external system boundary.*	P- "Communications are controlled at the external system boundary."
3.13.1[f]	*Communications are controlled at key internal boundaries.*	P- "Communications are controlled at key internal boundaries."
3.13.1[g]	*Communications are protected at the external system boundary.*	P- "Communications are protected at the external system boundary."

| 3.13.1[h] | Communications are protected at key internal boundaries. | P- "Communications are protected at key internal boundaries."

 ■ **This is where NIST 800-171A gets "granular" to a significant degree.** |

3.13.2 Employ architectural designs, software development techniques, and systems engineering principles that promote effective information security within organizational information systems.

MINIMUM/MORE COMPLETE ANSWER: Describing effective security architectural design measures can be as simple as the employment of a properly configured firewall or 2FA/MFA utilized by the company. It is highly likely that the average company seeking contracts with DOD will be specifically concerned with primary and secure architectures.

Other **mitigation** elements that can be described for this control may include physical security measures (e.g., a 24-hour guard force, reinforced fire doors, and cameras) or blacklist measures that prevent unauthorized applications from executing in the corporate network. See Control 3.13.10 for how 2FA operates internal or external to a company's network.

ASSESSMENT OBJECTIVE *Determine if:*		
SUB-CTRL	*DESCRIPTION*	**RECOMMENDED APPROACH**
3.13.2[a]	*Architectural designs that promote effective information security are identified.*	NCR/SSP-This includes firewalls, Intrusion Protection/Detection devices, etc.
3.13.2[b]	*Software development techniques that promote effective information security are identified.*	P- This requires that software development follows secure coding, scripting, etc., best

		practices, directions, and guidelines such as for DOD, Application Security Development (APPSECDEV) guidance.
3.13.2[c]	*Systems engineering principles that promote effective information security are identified.*	P- This requires that systems engineering follows secure engineering best practices.
3.13.2[d]	*Identified architectural designs that promote effective information security are employed.*	P- This requires that IT architecture and design follow secure engineering best practices.
3.13.2[e]	*Identified software development techniques that promote effective information security are employed.*	P- (See 3.13.2[b]) ■ Some of these control requirements may be reflected with third-party developers in the form of a contract.
3.13.2[f]	*Identified systems engineering principles that promote effective information security are employed.*	P- (See 3.13.2[c]) ■ Some of these control requirements may be reflected with third-party developers in the form of a contract.

Derived Security Requirements:

3.13.3 Separate user functionality from information system management functionality.

MINIMUM ANSWER: The policy should not allow privileged users to use the same credentials to access their users (e.g., email and Internet searches) and privileged user access. This separation of access is a basic network security principle and is intended to hamper both insider and external threats. (A suggested review of a similar control in Control 3.1.4, and its discussion of the **segregation of duty** principle for comparison.)

MORE COMPLETE ANSWER: There are technical solutions to automate this process. The product, for example, CyberArk ®, is used in many parts of the federal government to track and account for privileged user activity that is easily auditable. The ability to oversee, especially privileged user activity, should be readily audited and reviewed by senior company cybersecurity representatives.

ASSESSMENT OBJECTIVE *Determine if:*		
SUB-CTRL	*DESCRIPTION*	**RECOMMENDED APPROACH**
3.13.3[a]	*User functionality is identified.*	NCR
3.13.3[b]	*System management functionality is identified.*	NCR (This addresses functionality such as System, Database Administrators, etc.)
3.13.3[c]	*User functionality is separated from system management functionality.*	NCR

3.13.4 Prevent unauthorized and unintended information transfer via shared system resources.

MINIMUM ANSWER: **Peer-to-peer** networking is not authorized within the DOD, and it is strongly suggested the corporation's network also forbids its use. This is typically part of the AUP and should be enforceable to prevent, e.g., insider threat opportunities or used by external hackers to gain unauthorized access using legitimate employee security credentials.

MORE COMPLETE ANSWER: Suggest that this is part of the regular audit activity by designated IT personnel. They could be reviewing audit logs for unauthorized connections to include peer-to-peer networking.

3.13.5 Implement subnetworks for publicly accessible system components that are physically or logically separated from internal networks.

MINIMUM/MORE COMPLETE ANSWER: The most straightforward answer is that subnetworks reduce an intruder's ability to exploit corporate network addresses effectively. Have IT personnel establish subnetworks specifically for the email and webservers that are in the external Demilitarized Zone (DMZ) of the corporation's security boundary; see Control 3.14.2 for the location of a DMZ relative to the company's network. Some companies maintain external database servers; ensure they, too, have established subnetwork addresses.

ASSESSMENT OBJECTIVE Determine if:		
SUB-CTRL	DESCRIPTION	RECOMMENDED APPROACH
3.13.5[a]	Publicly accessible system components are identified.	NCR (Also should be part of SSP)
3.13.5[b]	Subnetworks for publicly accessible system components are physically or logically separated from internal networks.	NCR

3.13.6 Deny network communications traffic by default and allow network communications traffic by exception (i.e., deny all, permit by exception).

MINIMUM/MORE COMPLETE ANSWER: Like Control 3.4.8, this control can be selected by IT personnel. This is a technical control that should also be captured in the procedure document. These network settings are typically set at the firewall and involve **whitelisting** (only permitting access by exception) and **blacklisting** (from non-authorized Internet addresses) everyone else to enter the network. (Also, review Control 3.14.2).

ASSESSMENT OBJECTIVE Determine if:		
SUB-CTRL	DESCRIPTION	RECOMMENDED APPROACH
3.13.6[a]	Network communications traffic is denied by default.	NCR

| 3.13.6[b] | Network communications traffic is allowed by exception. | NCR |

3.13.7 Prevent remote devices from simultaneously establishing non-remote connections with the information system and communicating via some other connection to resources in external networks.

MINIMUM/MORE COMPLETE ANSWER: If a teleworking employee uses their remote device (i.e., notebook computer), and then connects to a non-remote (external) connection, it allows for an unauthorized external connection to exist; this provides a potential hacker with the ability to enter the network using the authorized employee's credentials.

It is critical that the company requires employees to use their VPN connection and blocks any insecure connections from accessing internal systems or applications. IT personnel need to ensure these settings are correctly configured and are part of the corporate cybersecurity procedure documentation.

3.13.8 Implement cryptographic mechanisms to prevent unauthorized disclosure of CUI during transmission unless otherwise protected by alternative physical safeguards.

MINIMUM ANSWER: Remember, this control is about external communications from the network and its system boundary. This is a DIT issue and is protected by the cryptographic solutions discussed earlier; see Control 3.1.3. Documentation should reflect the type and level of protection of data transmitted. Any additional protections such as a VPN, a secure circuit/dedicated circuit provided by a commercially contracted carrier, may afford more security for company data transmissions.

MORE COMPLETE ANSWER: Better levels of protection could be addressed regarding defense-in-depth, which is a current operational philosophy supported by DOD; additional layers of security provide extra defense. (See the "Defense-in-Depth" diagram at Control 3.14.2).

ASSESSMENT OBJECTIVE *Determine if:*		
SUB-CTRL	DESCRIPTION	RECOMMENDED APPROACH
3.13.8[a]	Cryptographic mechanisms intended to prevent unauthorized disclosure of CUI are identified.	NCR
3.13.8[b]	Alternative physical safeguards intended to prevent unauthorized disclosure of CUI are identified.	NCR
3.13.8[c]	Either cryptographic mechanisms or alternative physical safeguards are implemented to prevent unauthorized disclosure of CUI during transmission.	NCR

3.13.9 Terminate network connections associated with communications sessions at the end of the sessions or after a defined period of inactivity.

MINIMUM ANSWER: This was addressed in the AC control specific to the complete termination of a session. Sessions of suggested importance would be those such as to the financial, HR, or other essential computer server systems housing defined CUI/CDI. It is recommended that the procedure is explicitly updated to this control re-using language provided by any response to the control(s) discussing the termination of a network connection.

MORE COMPLETE ANSWER: Audit of sessions that have timed-out can strengthen this control. SA's and IT staff can determine from audit logs that the prescribed time-out period was met and enforced. Provide a sampling to any DOD inspector as part of the final packet.

ASSESSMENT OBJECTIVE *Determine if:*		
SUB-CTRL	*DESCRIPTION*	**RECOMMENDED APPROACH**
3.13.9[a]	A period of inactivity to terminate network connections associated with communications sessions is defined.	NCR
3.13.9[b]	Network connections associated with communications sessions are terminated at the end of the sessions.	NCR
3.13.9[c]	Network connections associated with communications sessions are terminated after the defined period of inactivity.	NCR

3.13.10 Establish and manage cryptographic keys for cryptography employed in the information system.

MINIMUM ANSWER: There are two significant scenarios likely to occur:

1. The use of commercial cryptographic programs that resides within the company's architecture or is provided by an external "managed service" provider is the most likely scenario. The keys will be maintained and secured by the cryptographic application. The company is establishing some form of 2FA solution. The public key would be secured somewhere else in the architecture, and the private key that of the employee would reside on a token such as CAC card or another critical device.

2. Using a DOD or other like 2FA solution with a CAC, Personal Identity Verification (PIV) card, or "token" such as those produced by RSA ® is likely if DOD authorizes the exchange of keys on its systems with that of the company. This requires a Certificate Authority (CA) usually outside the local network either managed by DOD or another trusted commercial entity with the capability to support "asymmetric" 2FA.

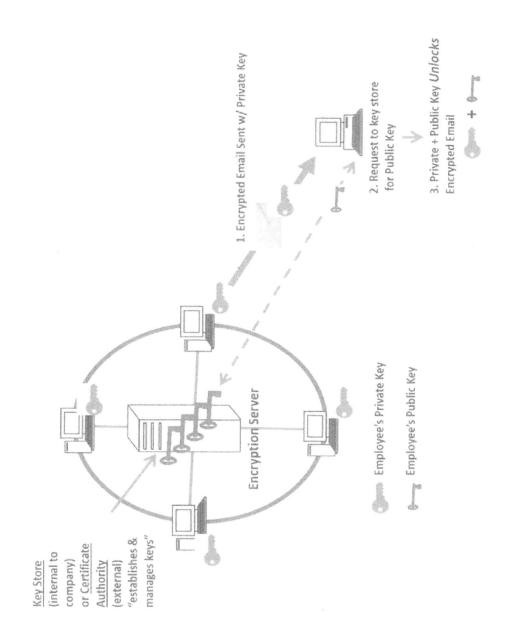

Two-factor Authentication (2FA) – Asymmetric Cryptography Basic Description

Whichever solution is used, ensure compatibility with DOD systems and other companies as part of its normal operations. ***All transmittal of CUI/CDI data is required to be encrypted.***

MORE COMPLETE ANSWER: Any more exceptional ability to secure and protect the **key store** within the company or through defined SLA's with outside service providers is essential. Ensure they have safeguards in place to protect unauthorized access to its system as well; they may use stronger encryption methods, but ensure they are recognized by DOD and are Federal Information Processing Standards (FIPS 140-2) compliant. (See Control 3.13.11 for identifying FIPS 140-2 solutions).

ASSESSMENT OBJECTIVE *Determine if:*		
SUB-CTRL	**DESCRIPTION**	**RECOMMENDED APPROACH**
3.13.10[a]	*Cryptographic keys are established whenever cryptography is employed.*	NCR
3.13.10[b]	*Cryptographic keys are managed whenever cryptography is employed.*	NCR

External Certification Authority Program (ECA)

In the case of DOD, the ECA program affords businesses the ability to interface with its 2FA infrastructure. The ECA supports the issuing of DoD-approved certificates to industry partners and other external third-party entities and organizations. The ECA program is designed to provide the mechanism for vendors to securely communicate with the DoD and authenticate to DoD Information Systems. It is expected to be further leveraged by other federal agencies as NIST 800-171 requirements expand beyond DOD.

For new vendors, the following instructions should be helpful when the ECA requirement becomes mandatory. To obtain a Public Key Infrastructure (PKI) ECA Medium Assurance Certificate (MAC), it will be most likely be obtained by two current significant vendors. The two vendors are: Either through the **Operational Research Consultants, Inc. (ORC)** at https://eca.orc.com/ or IdenTrust at http://www.identrust.com/certificates/eca/index.html). The certificate will come in three forms: Software (browser-based), token (preloaded USB device), or hardware (CAC card loaded).

The cost ranges from $100-$300 and is suitable from one to three years, depending on the selected option. When visiting these sites, ensure that the correct certificate is chosen. Select the "ECA/Identity certificate." On the IdenTrust web site, look for the Medium Assurance Certificate.

The process will take from one to two weeks to receive the certificate. The certificate will be provided by email with instructions on how to download the certificate. Once the certificate is received, contact the Contract Office to determine what help desk will need to be communicated to request account establishment on the respective federal IT infrastructure. It will typically require at least 30 minutes to 1 hour to create the account but expect longer with non-DOD federal agencies.

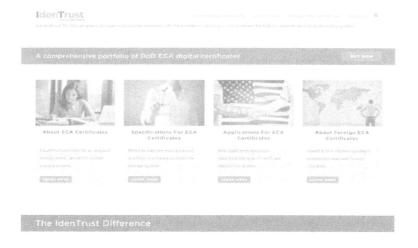

IdenTrust DOD ECA Program Site

3.13.11 Employ FIPS-validated cryptography when used to protect the confidentiality of CUI.

MINIMUM/MORE COMPLETE ANSWER: The company needs to confirm that its encryption applications are FIPS 140-2 compliant. It can easily be verified at the website below:

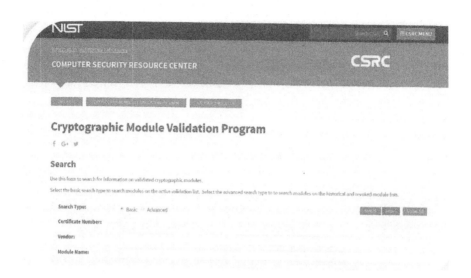

Official NIST site to confirm FIPS 140-2 cryptographic compliance[17]
(https://csrc.nist.gov/projects/cryptographic-module-validation-program/validated-modules/search)

3.13.12 Prohibit remote activation of collaborative computing devices and provide indication of devices in use to users present at the device.

MINIMUM ANSWER: Collaborative computing devices include, for example, "networked whiteboards, cameras, and microphones." The intent is to prevent these devices from being used by intruders to conduct reconnaissance of a network.

This can be prevented by changes in registry settings that only authorized IT personnel with privileged access can change. Furthermore, if these items are active, visible lighting or audible alerts should be considered to notify IT and security personnel. The policy should require that individuals do not change these settings to include privileged users. Any change should only be approved by exception and require a privileged user who is authorized to make such changes.

MORE COMPLETE ANSWER: Auditing and SIEM solutions could be configured to ensure these settings are not tampered. See Control 3.3.2 for further discussion of this topic area.

---

[17] NOTE: FIPS 140-2 expires in 2021 and will be replaced by FIPS 140-3.

ASSESSMENT OBJECTIVE Determine if:		
SUB-CTRL	DESCRIPTION	RECOMMENDED APPROACH
3.13.12 [a]	Collaborative computing devices are identified.	NCR
3.13.12 [b]	Collaborative computing devices provide indication to users of devices in use.	NCR
3.13.12 [c]	Remote activation of collaborative computing devices is prohibited.	P - "Remote activation of collaborative computing devices is prohibited."

3.13.13 Control and monitor the use of mobile code.

MINIMUM/MORE COMPLETE ANSWER: Mobile code is mainly part of Internet-capable business phones. The company's phone carrier can limit the types and kinds of mobile applications that reside on employee phones. Most applications are usually required to meet secure industry development standards. It is best to confirm with the company's carrier how mobile code apps are secured and restrict employees to a set number of approved mobile apps. Define in the company procedures the base applications provided to each employee, and the process for work-specific applications that other specialists in the company require.

ASSESSMENT OBJECTIVE Determine if:		
SUB-CTRL	DESCRIPTION	RECOMMENDED APPROACH
3.13.13[a]	Use of mobile code is controlled.	P – "Use of mobile code is controlled." (Restricted through a carrier and must be approved by the company or agency authorized

		representative before accessible by employees).
3.13.13[b]	*Use of mobile code is monitored.*	P – *"Use of mobile code is monitored."* (Reports provided on an established/contractual basis).

3.13.14 Control and monitor the use of Voice over Internet Protocol (VoIP) technologies.

MINIMUM ANSWER: The most likely current place VOIP would exist is the company's phone service. Ensure with the phone carrier that their VOIP services are secure and what level of security is used to protect corporate communications. Furthermore, identify any contract information that provides details about the provided security.

MORE COMPLETE ANSWER: Verify what monitoring services and network protection (from malware, viruses, etc.) are part of the current service plan. If necessary, determine whether both the control and monitoring are included or extra services. If not fully covered, consider formulating a POAM.

ASSESSMENT OBJECTIVE *Determine if:*		
SUB-CTRL	*DESCRIPTION*	RECOMMENDED APPROACH
3.13.14[a]	*Use of Voice over Internet Protocol (VoIP) technologies is controlled.*	NCR (See sub-control 3.13.13[a] for a similar discussion)
3.13.14[b]	*Use of Voice over Internet Protocol (VoIP) technologies is monitored.*	NCR

3.13.15 Protect the authenticity of communications sessions.

MINIMUM/ MORE COMPLETE ANSWER: This control addresses communications' protection and establishes confidence that the session is authentic; it ensures the identity of the individual and the information being transmitted. Authenticity protection includes, for example, protecting against session hijacking or insertion of false information.

This can be resolved by some form, hard or soft token MFA/2FA, solution. It will ensure the identity and FIPS 140-2 encryption to prevent data manipulation. See Control 3.5.2 for further discussion. While these are not complete solutions, they significantly demonstrate more certainty that the communications are authentic.

3.13.16 Protect the confidentiality of CUI at rest.
MINIMUM ANSWER: This is a DAR issue, and as discussed earlier, it is a DOD requirement. Ensure the proper software package is procured that meets FIPS 140-2 standards. (See Control 3.13.11 for NIST's website information).

MORE COMPLETE ANSWER: If using a CSP, ensure it is using DOD accepted FIPS 140-2 standards; it will make authorization simpler. Moreover, a reminder, if the business cannot use FIPS 140-2 solutions, ensures an effective POAM is developed that addresses why it cannot be currently implemented and when the company is prepared to implement the control. *When will the company be compliant?*

SYSTEM AND INFORMATION INTEGRITY (SI)
Anti-virus and Anti-Malware

This control family is about maintaining the integrity of data within the company's system security boundary. It primarily defended by active measures such as anti-virus and malware protection. This control addresses the establishment of procedures for the effective implementation of the security controls. Cybersecurity policies and procedures may include Information Security (INFOSEC) policies. Company risk management strategy is a crucial factor in establishing decisive system protections.

Basic Security Requirements:

3.14.1 Identify, report, and correct information and information system flaws in a timely manner.
MINIMUM ANSWER: This control addresses what are considered security-relevant flaws. These would include, for example, software patches, hotfixes, anti-virus, and anti-malware signatures.

Typically, network Operating Systems can check with manufacturers via the Internet for updated, e.g., "security patches" in near-real-time. It is essential to allow patches from the authorized manufacturers and sources to be updated as soon as possible. They usually are designed to fix bugs and minor through significant security vulnerabilities. The sooner the system is updated, the better. Ensure a process, such as checks by IT personnel at least twice a day. Many systems will allow for automated "pushes" to the network. Ensure that documented processes account for review by IT personnel to "audit" known pushes by only authorized sources.

Major DOD Security Events/Zero-Day Attacks: There are times that the federal government becomes aware of **zero-day attacks**. These are attacks where there is no current security patch and sometimes requires other actions by DOD supported organizations and corporations; be mindful of these events from DOD and Department of Homeland Security (DHS) alerts. These will require near-immediate action. Furthermore, DOD may direct everyone, including NIST 800-171 authorized businesses, to report their status to the Contract Officer by an established deadline.

MORE COMPLETE ANSWER: Ensure that designated IT personnel are aware of and are monitoring the active vulnerabilities sites from both DOD and DHS. An active process to verify the current state of threats against DOD is an excellent means to establish a company's due diligence in this area.

DHS's United States Computer Emergency Readiness Team (US-CERT) has the latest information on vulnerabilities to include zero-day updates. It is also recommended that designated IT personnel sign up for the Rich Site Summary (RSS) data feeds by selecting the symbol to the left. The address for the overall site is: https://www.us-cert.gov/ncas/current-activity

ASSESSMENT OBJECTIVE *Determine if:*		
SUB-CTRL	DESCRIPTION	RECOMMENDED APPROACH
3.14.1[a]	The time within which to identify system flaws is specified.	P – Suggested: "Upon notification from X or upon the recognition that software patches or hotfixes are out of date, anti-virus and anti-malware signatures are not current, etc.
3.14.1[b]	System flaws are identified within the specified time frame.	P- This, at a minimum, should be upon recognition and a process that is in place to identify when reviews should occur, typically, weekly.
3.14.1[c]	The time within which to report system flaws is specified.	P – (See above)
3.14.1[d]	System flaws are reported within the specified time frame.	P – (See above)
3.14.1[e]	The time within which to correct system flaws is specified.	P- Flaws should be addressed immediately or within 24 hours, typically. Where a patch, for example, harms

		operations, there need to be roll-back procedures. This should then require a POAM be documented with a possible waiver if the change is too negative.
3.14.1[f]	*System flaws are corrected within the specified time frame.*	P – (See 4.14.1[f])

3.14.2 Provide protection from malicious code at appropriate locations within organizational information systems.

MINIMUM ANSWER: Protecting the network from malicious code is typically through both active anti-virus and malware protection applications or services. Ensure if additional protections provided by the businesses' commercial ISP are included in any artifact submission.

MORE COMPLETE ANSWER: Any additional protections could be provided by "smart" firewalls, routers, and switches. Specific commercial devices provide extra defenses.

Smart Firewalls. Smart firewalls include standard protection capabilities. Additionally, firewalls, specifically, can afford whitelisting and blacklisting protections.

- **Whitelisting** can be used only to allow authorized outside users on an internal Access Control List (ACL). The ACL needs to be managed actively to ensure that legitimate organizations can communicate through the businesses' firewall. The external interested business or organizations can still communicate with the business for some services like the company web site and email system that resides in what is termed the Demilitarized Zone (DMZ). Whitelisting is typically implemented at the firewall. See the Diagram below.

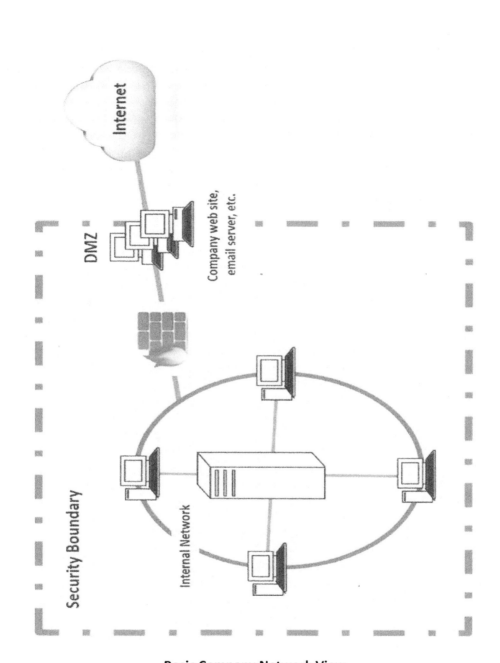

Basic Company Network View

- **Blacklisting** is used to block known "bad guys." There are companies and the DOD that can provide lists of known malicious sites based upon their Internet addresses. Blacklists require continuous management to be most effective.

Both solutions are not guaranteed. While they afford additional means to slow hackers and nation-state intruders, they are not total solutions. Therefore DOD, and much of the cybersecurity community, strongly supports the principle of **defense in depth** where other technological solutions help to reinforce the protections because of security programming flaws inadvertently created by software developers and the constant challenge of hackers exploiting various areas of modern IT architectures to conduct their nefarious actions.

The Principle of Defense in Depth

ASSESSMENT OBJECTIVE		
Determine if:		
SUB-CTRL	***DESCRIPTION***	**RECOMMENDED APPROACH**
3.14.2[a]	*Designated locations for malicious code protection are identified.*	P/SSP – Should identify the application and mechanisms within the architecture devoted to malicious code identification.
3.14.2[b]	*Protection from malicious code at designated locations is provided.*	P/SSP – (Same as 3.14.2[a])

3.14.3 Monitor information system security alerts and advisories and take appropriate actions in response.

MINIMUM ANSWER: This SI control can be best met through auditing. This can be achieved by using applications (such as anti-virus) or tools embedded within the architecture. These should include Intrusion Detection capabilities, network packet capture tools such as Wireshark ®, or audit logs. The process and associated actions should consist of recognition and notification to senior management. Management should ensure developed methods define when an event is raised to a level of a notifiable incident to DOD.

MORE COMPLETE ANSWER: A more-complete solution could use other advanced toolsets based on the education and experience of the IT support staff. These could include malicious code protection software (such as found in more advanced anti-malware solutions). Consideration should always include the overall ROI for the investment in such tools.

If the company can only implement minor portions of the control and has the planned intent to invest in improved tools in the future, it is best to develop a well-defined POAM with achievable milestones for the company to pursue. It will demonstrate to DOD a commitment to improving cybersecurity vice ignoring other technical methods to reduce the risk to the company and its associated CUI/CDI.

ASSESSMENT OBJECTIVE		
Determine if:		
SUB-CTRL	*DESCRIPTION*	**RECOMMENDED APPROACH**
3.14.3[a]	*Response actions to system security alerts and advisories are identified.*	P – This would align with the Incident Response Plan (IRP); (See IR 3.6 Controls)
3.14.3[b]	*System security alerts and advisories are monitored.*	P – This would identify who monitors; small companies may include SA's and larger companies with use their Security Operations Center (SOC) watch personnel
3.14.3[c]	*Actions in response to system security alerts and advisories are taken.*	P – Part of IRP and designated personnel.

Derived Security Requirements:

3.14.4 Update malicious code protection mechanisms when new releases are available.
MINIMUM/COMPLETE ANSWER: This is usually quickly resolved through ongoing software license agreements with vendors for malicious code internal programs or external contracted support services. Assuming a new version is made available during the active period of the license, updates are typically free; document the company's procedure for maintaining not only current but legal versions of malicious code detection and prevention software or services.

3.14.5 Perform periodic scans of the information system and real-time scans of files from external sources as files are downloaded, opened, or executed.
MINIMUM ANSWER: Many of the solutions already discussed afford real-time scanning of files and traffic as they traverse the network. Scanning of files should always be

conducted from external downloads for both viruses and malware. Ensure the technical policy settings are always set to perform real-time scans of the network, endpoints (i.e., work computers both internal and used by teleworking employees), and files entering the network by the appropriate tools to ensure network operation and security.

MORE COMPLETE ANSWER: Require IT personnel to regularly check that real-time scanning has not been changed accidentally or on purpose. It is essential to be aware that potential intruders will attempt to shut down any security features such as active scanning. Train IT personnel to manually check at least weekly and alert management if the changes are suspicious. Identifying possible entry into the company's data is a function of the SI as well as a significant component of the AU control family.

ASSESSMENT OBJECTIVE *Determine if:*		
SUB-CTRL	DESCRIPTION	RECOMMENDED APPROACH
3.14.5[a]	The frequency for malicious code scans is defined.	NCR – Recommended: real-time using approved malware detection software; otherwise, at least daily for smaller operations (not recommended until the tool is purchased and deployed)
3.14.5[b]	Malicious code scans are performed with the defined frequency.	NCR
3.14.5[c]	Real-time malicious code scans of files from external sources as files are downloaded, opened, or executed are performed.	NCR

3.14.6 Monitor the information system including inbound and outbound communications traffic, to detect attacks and indicators of potential attacks.
MINIMUM ANSWER: As discussed, anti-virus and malware provide some level of checking of inbound and outbound traffic. Document both manual and automated means to ensure traffic is monitored.

Procedures should identify the people who will conduct the regular review, the process that ensures proper oversight is in place to identify violations of this control, and what technologies are being used to protect inbound and outbound traffic from attack. (See Control 3.6.1 for discussion about the PPT Model, and its application to address security controls).

MORE COMPLETE ANSWER: This could also identify commercial ISP's supporting the business with "trusted" connections to the Internet. Refer to provided SLA's and provided contact information for the DOD review.

ASSESSMENT OBJECTIVE		
Determine if:		
SUB-CTRL	*DESCRIPTION*	RECOMMENDED APPROACH
3.14.6[a]	*The system is monitored to detect attacks and indicators of potential attacks.*	NCR
3.14.6[b]	*Inbound communications traffic is monitored to detect attacks and indicators of potential attacks.*	NCR
3.14.6[c]	*Outbound communications traffic is monitored to detect attacks and indicators of potential attacks.*	NCR

3.14.7 Identify unauthorized use of the information system.
MINIMUM ANSWER: This is met through active and regular auditing of, for example, systems, applications, intrusion detections, and firewall logs. It is essential to recognize that there may be limitations for the IT staff to properly and adequately review all available logs created by the company's IT network. It is best to identify the critical logs

to review regularly and any secondary logs as time permits. Avoid trying to review all available system logs; there are many. Also, determine the level of effort required processing time, ability, and training of the company's' IT support staff.

MORE COMPLETE ANSWER: In addition to the above, consider third-party companies that can provide a monitoring service of the network. While these may be expensive, it will depend on the business, its mission, and the critically of the data. This solution will require a well-developed SLA's with appropriate oversight to ensure the company receives the Quality of Service (QOS) the company needs.

ASSESSMENT OBJECTIVE *Determine if:*		
SUB-CTRL	**DESCRIPTION**	**RECOMMENDED APPROACH**
3.14.7[a]	*Authorized use of the system is defined.*	NCR
3.14.7[b]	*Unauthorized use of the system is identified.*	NCR

MATURITY IS A MATTER OF CONTROL IMPLEMENTATION

Maturity of security control implementation is more than a one-time evaluation of the 110 controls listed in NIST 800-171 (or any of the other major cybersecurity protection frameworks.)It relies on continuous monitoring and active oversight of changes in the IT environment. Too many "cybersecurity experts" have never run an ATO, scanned for missing patches, or verified a security policy—we have too many "posers" and senior leaders blinded by their lack of knowledge about risk management in general. Until we enforce oversight at all levels, even the CMMC is doomed to fail. Let us get truly serious about the cyber-threats pounding at our IT perimeter hourly.

The premise of the NIST cybersecurity process is to recognize that it is not about absolute certainty. Weak or poorly implemented security controls will not stop cyber-attacks. The foundation of risk management is about knowing the system's overall weaknesses. It is about the company's leadership, not just the IT staff, has identified where those weaknesses exist.

Risk Management is about a defined Continuous Monitoring (ConMon) procedures and effective Risk Assessment processes. Proper processes afford the needed protection to a company's or organization's sensitive CUI/CDI. The 110 NIST 800-171 controls are not meant to be complete answers to an ever-changing risk landscape. It is only through an active and continual review of the controls can DOD and companies ensure with near-certainty their networks are as secure *as possible.*

This manual provides a moderate understanding of the controls, how to effectively respond to them, and meet NIST 800-171 requirements to authorize a company to conduct business with the DOD. While DOD may be the first federal agency to mandate NIST 800-171 implementation, expect other agencies such as the Department of Homeland Security (DHS), the Department of Commerce (DOC), home of NIST, and Department of Energy (DOE), to be the next likely candidates to necessitate businesses to meet NIST 800-171.

The main objective of this manual is to provide a plain-English and how-to guide for the non-IT business owner. The target of this book is to provide information about the DIB, and their IT staffs can critically think about how to best respond to cyber-threats. This book provides a serious starting point for small through big business to not only meet the requirements of NIST 800-171, but to truly protect its computers, systems, and data from the "bad guys" near and far.

APPENDIX A -- RELEVANT REFERENCES

Federal Information Security Modernization Act of 2014 (P.L. 113-283), December 2014.
http://www.gpo.gov/fdsys/pkg/PLAW-113publ283/pdf/PLAW-113publ283.pdf

Executive Order 13556, *Controlled Unclassified Information*, November 2010.
http://www.gpo.gov/fdsys/pkg/FR-2010-11-09/pdf/2010-28360.pdf

Executive Order 13636, *Improving Critical Infrastructure Cybersecurity*, February 2013.
http://www.gpo.gov/fdsys/pkg/FR-2013-02-19/pdf/2013-03915.pdf

National Institute of Standards and Technology Federal Information Processing Standards Publication 200 (as amended), *Minimum Security Requirements for Federal Information and Information Systems*.
http://csrc.nist.gov/publications/fips/fips200/FIPS-200-final-march.pdf

National Institute of Standards and Technology Special Publication 800-53 (as amended), *Security and Privacy Controls for Federal Information Systems and Organizations*.
http://dx.doi.org/10.6028/NIST.SP.800-53r4

National Institute of Standards and Technology Special Publication 800-171, rev. 1, *Protecting Controlled Unclassified Information in Nonfederal Information Systems and Organizations.* https://nvlpubs.nist.gov/nistpubs/SpecialPublications/NIST.SP.800-171r1.pdf

National Institute of Standards and Technology Special Publication 800-171A, *Assessing Security Requirements for Controlled Unclassified Information*
https://csrc.nist.gov/CSRC/media/Publications/sp/800-171a/draft/sp800-171A-draft.pdf

National Institute of Standards and Technology *Framework for Improving Critical Infrastructure Cybersecurity* (as amended).
http://www.nist.gov/cyberframework

APPENDIX B -- TERMS & GLOSSARY

Audit log. A chronological record of information system activities, including records of system accesses and operations performed in a given period.

Authentication. Verifying the identity of a user, process, or device, often as a prerequisite to allowing access to resources in an information system.

Availability. Ensuring timely and reliable access to and use of information.

Baseline Configuration. A documented set of specifications for an information system, or a configuration item within a system, that has been formally reviewed and agreed on at a given point in time, and which can be changed only through change control procedures.

Blacklisting. The process used to identify: (i) software programs that are not authorized to execute on an information system; or (ii) prohibited websites.

Confidentiality. Preserving authorized restrictions on information access and disclosure, including means for protecting personal privacy and proprietary information.

Configuration Management. A collection of activities focused on establishing and maintaining the integrity of information technology products and information systems, through control of processes for initializing, changing, and monitoring the configurations of those products and systems throughout the system development life cycle.

Controlled Unclassified Information (CUI/CDI).

Information that law, regulation, or governmentwide policy requires to have safeguarding or disseminating controls, excluding information that is classified under Executive Order 13526, Classified National Security Information, December 29, 2009, or any predecessor or successor order, or the Atomic Energy Act of 1954, as amended.

External network. A network not controlled by the company.

FIPS-validated cryptography. A cryptographic module validated by the Cryptographic Module Validation Program (CMVP) to meet requirements specified in FIPS Publication 140-2 (as amended). As a prerequisite to CMVP validation, the cryptographic module is required to employ a cryptographic algorithm implementation that has successfully passed validation testing by the Cryptographic Algorithm Validation Program (CAVP).

Hardware. The physical components of an information system.

Incident. An occurrence that actually or potentially jeopardizes the confidentiality, integrity, or availability of an information system or the information the system processes, stores, or transmits or that constitutes a violation or imminent threat of violation of security policies, security procedures, or acceptable use policies.

Information Security. The protection of information and information systems from unauthorized access, use, disclosure, disruption, modification, or destruction to provide confidentiality, integrity, and availability.

Information System. A discrete set of information resources organized for the collection, processing, maintenance, use, sharing, dissemination, or disposition of information.

Information Technology. Any equipment or interconnected system or subsystem of equipment that is used in the automatic acquisition, storage, manipulation, management, movement, control, display, switching, interchange, transmission, or reception of data or information by the executive agency. It includes computers, ancillary equipment, software, firmware, and similar procedures, services (including support services), and related resources.

Integrity. Guarding against improper information modification or destruction and includes ensuring information non-repudiation and authenticity.

Internal Network. A network where: (i) the establishment, maintenance, and provisioning of security controls are under the direct control of organizational employees or contractors; or (ii) cryptographic encapsulation or similar security technology implemented between organization-controlled endpoints, provides the same effect (at least concerning confidentiality and integrity).

Malicious Code. Software intended to perform an unauthorized process that will hurt the confidentiality, integrity, or availability of an information system; a virus, worm, Trojan horse, or other code-based entity that infects a host. Spyware and some forms of adware are also examples of malicious code.

Media. Physical devices or writing surfaces including, but not limited to, magnetic tapes, optical disks, magnetic disks, and printouts (but not including display media) onto which information is recorded, stored or printed within an information system.

Mobile Code. Software programs or parts of programs obtained from remote information systems, transmitted across a network, and executed on a local information system without explicit installation or execution by the recipient.

Mobile device. A portable computing device that: (i) has a small form factor such that a single individual can easily carry it; (ii) is designed to operate without a physical connection (e.g., wirelessly transmit or receive information); (iii) possesses local, nonremovable or removable data storage; and (iv) includes a self-contained power source. Mobile devices may also include voice communication capabilities, on-board sensors that allow the devices to capture information or built-in features for synchronizing local data with remote locations. Examples include smartphones, tablets, and E-readers.

Multifactor Authentication. Authentication using two or more different factors to achieve authentication. Factors include: (i) something you know (e.g., password/PIN); (ii) something you have (e.g., cryptographic identification device, token); or (iii) something you are (e.g., biometric).

Nonfederal Information System. An information system that does not meet the criteria for a federal information system. Nonfederal organization.

Network. Information system(s) implemented with a collection of interconnected components. Such components may include routers, hubs, cabling, telecommunications controllers, key distribution centers, and technical control devices.

Portable storage device. An information system component that can be inserted into and removed from an information system, and that is used to store data or information (e.g., text, video, audio, or image data). Such components are typically implemented on magnetic, optical, or solid-state devices (e.g., floppy disks, compact/digital video disks, flash/thumb drives, external hard disk drives, and flash memory cards/drives that contain nonvolatile memory).

Privileged Account. An information system account with authorizations of a privileged user.

Privileged User. A user that is authorized (and therefore, trusted) to perform security-relevant functions that ordinary users are not authorized to perform.

Remote Access. Access to an organizational information system by a user (or a process acting on behalf of a user) communicating through an external network (e.g., the Internet).

Risk. A measure of the extent to which a potential circumstance or event threaten an entity, and typically a function of (i) the adverse impacts that would arise if the time or event occurs; and (ii) the likelihood of occurrence. Information system-related security risks are those risks that arise from the loss of confidentiality, integrity, or availability of information or information systems and reflect the potential adverse impacts to organizational operations (including mission, functions, image, or reputation), organizational assets, individuals, other organizations, and the Nation.

Sanitization.	Actions were taken to render data written on media unrecoverable by both ordinary and, for some forms of sanitization, extraordinary means. The process of removing information from media such that data recovery is not possible. It includes removing all classified labels, markings, and activity logs.
Security Control.	A safeguard or countermeasure prescribed for an information system or an organization designed to protect the confidentiality, integrity, and availability of its information and to meet a set of defined security requirements.
Security Control Assessment.	The testing or evaluation of security controls to determine the extent to which the controls are implemented correctly, operating as intended, and producing the desired outcome concerning meeting the security requirements for an information system or organization.
Security Functions.	The hardware, software, or firmware of the information system responsible for enforcing the system security policy and supporting the isolation of code and data on which the protection is based.
Threat.	Any circumstance or event with the potential to adversely impact organizational operations (including mission, functions, image, or reputation), organizational assets, individuals, other organizations, or the Nation through an information system via unauthorized access, destruction, disclosure, modification of information, or denial of service.
Whitelisting.	The process used to identify: (i) software programs that are authorized to execute an information system.

APPENDIX C – CONTINUOUS MONITORING: *A More Detailed Discussion*

NOTE: CM in this article is about Continuous Monitoring (ConMon) activities discussed in greater depth; it should not be confused with discussion in this book regarding Configuration Management.

Continuous Monitoring: A More Detailed Discussion

Cybersecurity is not about shortcuts. There are no easy solutions to years of leaders demurring their responsibility to address the growing threats in cyberspace. We hoped that the Office of Personnel Management (OPM) breach several years ago would herald the needed focus, energy, and funding to quash the bad-guys. That has proven an empty hope where leaders have abrogated their responsibility to lead in cyberspace. The "holy grail" solution of Continuous Monitoring (CM) has been the most misunderstood solution where too many shortcuts are perpetrated by numerous federal agencies and the private sector to create an illusion of success. This paper is specifically written to help leaders better understand what constitutes an accurate statement of: "we have continuous monitoring." This is not about shortcuts. This is about education, training, and understanding at the highest leadership levels that cybersecurity is not a technical issue, but a leadership issue.

The Committee on National Security Systems defines CM as: "[t]he processes implemented to maintain current security status for one or more information systems on which the operational mission of the enterprise depends," (CNSS, 2010). CM has been described as the holistic solution of end-to-end cybersecurity coverage and the answer to providing an effective global Risk Management (RM) solution. It promises the elimination of the 3-year recertification cycle that has been the bane of cybersecurity professionals.

For CM to become a reality for any agency, it must meet the measures and expectations as defined in National Institute of Standards and Technology (NIST) Special Publication (SP) 800-137, Information Security Continuous Monitoring for Federal Information Systems and Organizations. "Continuous monitoring has evolved as a best practice for managing risk on an ongoing basis," (SANS Institute, 2016); it is an instrument that supports effective, continual, and recurring RM assurances. For any agency to indeed espouse it has attained full CM compliance, it must be able to coordinate all the described major elements as found in NIST SP 800-137.

CM is not just the passive visibility pieces, but also includes the active efforts of vulnerability scanning, threat alert, reduction, mitigation, or elimination of a dynamic Information Technology (IT) environment. The Department of Homeland Security (DHS) has couched its approach to CM more holistically. Their program to protect government networks is more aptly called: "Continuous Diagnostics and Monitoring" or CDM and includes a need to react to an active network attacker. "The ability to make IT networks, end-points and applications visible; to identify malicious activity; and, to respond [emphasis added] immediately is critical to defending information systems and networks," (Sann, 2016).

Another description of CM can be found in NIST's CAESARS Framework Extension: An Enterprise Continuous Monitoring Technical Reference Model (Second Draft). It defines its essential characteristics within the concept of "Continuous Security Monitoring." It is described as a "…risk management approach to Cybersecurity that maintains a picture of an organization's security posture, provides visibility into assets, leverages use of automated data feeds, monitors effectiveness of security controls, and enables prioritization of remedies," (NIST, 2012); it must demonstrate visibility, data feeds, measures of effectiveness and allow for solutions. It provides another description of what should be shown to ensure full CM designation under the NIST standard.

The government's Federal Risk and Authorization Management Program (Fed-RAMP) has defined similar CM goals. These objectives are all key outcomes of a successful CM implementation. Its "… goal[s]…[are] to provide: (i) operational visibility; (ii) annual self-attestation on security control implementations; (iii) managed change control; (iv) and attendance to incident response duties," (GSA, 2012). These objectives, while not explicit to NIST SP 800-37, are well-aligned with the desires of an effective and complete solution.

RMF creates the structure and documentation needs of CM; CM represents the specific implementation and oversight of Information Security (IS) within an IT environment. It supports the general activity of RM within an agency. (See Figure 1 below). The RMF "… describes a disciplined and structured process that integrates information security and risk management activities into the system development life cycle" (NIST-B, 2011). RMF is the structure that both describes and relies upon CM as its risk oversight and effective mechanism between IS and RM.

Figure 1. CM "bridges" Information Security and Risk Management

This article provides a conceptual framework to address how an agency would approach identifying a correct CM solution through NIST SP 800-137. It discusses the additional need to align component requirements with the *"11 Security Automation Domains"* that are necessary to implement true CM. (See Figure 2 below). It is through the complete implementation and

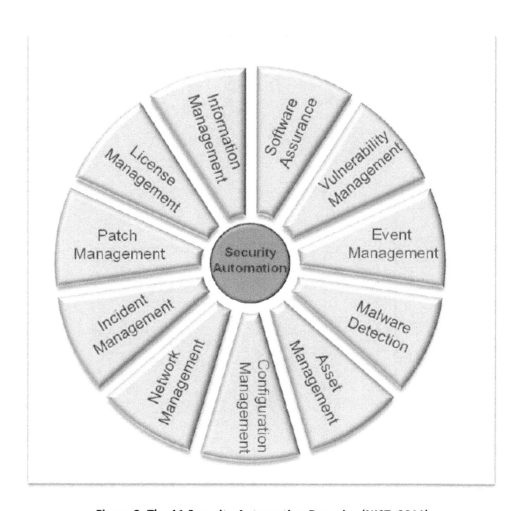

Figure 2. The 11 Security Automation Domains (NIST, 2011)

integration with the other described components—See Figure 3 below--that an organization can correctly state it has achieved CM.

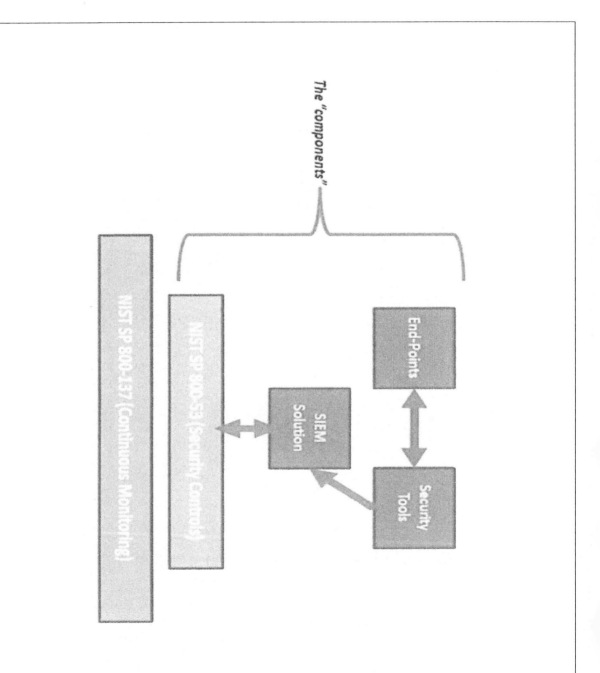

Figure 3. The "Components" of an Effective Continuous Monitoring

Continuous Monitoring – First Generation

For CM to be effective and genuine, it must align end-point visibility with security monitoring tools. This includes security monitoring tools with connectivity to "end-points" such as laptops, desktops, servers, routers, firewalls, etc. Additionally, these must work with a highly integrated Security Information and Event Management (SIEM) device. The other "component" is a clear linkage between the end-points, security monitoring tools, and the SIEM appliance, working with the *Security Automation Domains* (See Figure 2). These would include, for example, the areas of malware detection, asset, and event management. CM must first address these composite components to create a "First Generation" instantiation.

More specifically, a SIEM appliance provides the central core data processing capabilities to effectively coordinate all the inputs and outputs from across the IT enterprise. It manages the data integration and interpretation of all CM components. Moreover, it provides the necessary visibility and intelligence for an active incident response capability.

In describing a *First Generation* implementation, the following arithmetic expression is offered:

> END-POINTS $_{\text{VISIBILITY}}$ + SECURITY TOOLS $_{\text{MONITORING}}$ +
> SECURITY CONTROLS $_{\text{ALIGNMENT}}$ → (INPUT) SIEM SOLUTION →
> 11 SECURITY AUTOMATION DOMAINS $_{\text{COMPARISON}}$ →
> (OUTPUT) [VISIBILITY + ANALYSIS + ALERTS] = CM $_{\text{FIRST GEN}}$

An Arithmetic Expression for First-Generation Continuous Monitoring

End-point devices must be persistently visible to the applicable security devices. Together, these parts must align with the respective security controls, as described in NIST SP 800-53. The selected SIEM tool must be able to accept these inputs and analyze them against defined security policy settings, recurring vulnerability scans, signature-based threats, and heuristic/activity-based analyses to ensure the environment's security posture. The outputs of the SIEM must support the further visibility of the IT environment, conduct and disseminate vital intelligence, and alert leadership to any ongoing or imminent dangers. The expression above is designed to provide a conceptual representation of the cybersecurity professional attempting to ascertain effective CM implementation or to develop a complete CM answer for an agency or corporation.

Additionally, the SIEM must distribute data feeds in near-real-time to analysts and critical leaders. It provides for multi-level "dashboard" data streams and issues alert based upon prescribed policy settings. Once these base, First Generation functionalities are consistently aligning with the Security Automation Domains, then an organization or corporation can definitively express it meets the requirements of CM.

End-Points

It is necessary to identify hardware and software configuration items that must be known and constantly traceable before implementing CM within an enterprise IT environment. End-point visibility is not the hardware devices, but the baseline software of each hardware device on the network.

Configuration Management is also a foundational requirement for any organization's security posture. Soundly implemented Configuration Management must be the basis of any complete CM implementation. At the beginning of any IS effort, cyber-professionals must know the current "as-is" hardware and software component state within the enterprise. End-points must be protected and monitored because they are the most valuable target for would-be hackers and cyber-thieves.

Configuration Management provides the baseline that establishes a means to identify potential compromise between the enterprise's end-points and the requisite security tools. "Organizations with a robust and effective [Configuration Management] process need to consider information security implications concerning the development and operation of information systems including hardware, software, applications, and documentation," (NIST-A, 2011).

The RMF requires the categorization of systems and data as high, moderate, or low regarding risk. The Federal Information Processing Standards (FIPS) Publication 199 methodology is typically used to establish data sensitivity levels in the federal government. FIPS 199 aids the cybersecurity professional in determining data protection standards of both end-points and the data stored in these respective parts. For example, a system that collects and retains sensitive data, such as financial information, requires a higher level of security. End-points must be recognized as repositories of highly valued data to cyber-threats.

Further, cyber-security professionals must be constantly aware of the "...administrative and technological costs of offering a high degree of protection for all federal systems..." (Ross, Katzke, & Toth, 2005). This is not a matter of recognizing the physical end-point alone, but the value and associated costs of the virtual data stored, monitored, and protected continually. FIPS 199 assists system owners in determining whether a higher level of protection is warranted, with higher associated costs, based upon an overall FIPS 199 evaluation.

Security Tools

Security monitoring tools must identify in near-real-time an active threat. Examples include anti-virus or anti-malware applications used to monitor network and end-point activities. Products like McAfee and Symantec provide enterprise capabilities that help to identify and reduce threats.

Other security tools would address in whole or part the remaining NIST Security Automation Domains. These would include, for example, tools to provide asset visibility, vulnerability detection, patch management updates, etc. However, it is also critical to recognize that even the best current security tools are not necessarily capable of defending against all attacks. New malware or zero-day attacks pose continual challenges to the cybersecurity workforce.

For example, DHS's EINSTEIN system would not have stopped the 2015 Office of Personnel Management breach. Even DHS's latest iteration of EINSTEIN, EINSTEIN 3, an advanced network monitoring and response system designed to protect federal governments' networks, would not have stopped that attack. "…EINSTEIN 3 would not have been able to catch a threat that [had] no known footprints, according to multiple industry experts" (Sternstein, 2015).

Not until there are a much higher integration and availability of cross-cutting intelligence and more capable security tools can any single security tool ever be entirely useful. The need for multiple security monitoring tools that provide "defense in depth" may be a better protective strategy. However, with various tools monitoring the same Security Automation Domains, such an approach will undoubtedly increase the costs of maintaining a secure agency or corporate IT environment. A determination of Return on Investment (ROI) balanced against a well-defined threat risk scoring approach is further needed at all levels of the federal and corporate IT workspace.

Security Controls

"Organizations are required to adequately mitigate the risk arising from the use of information and information systems in the execution of missions and business functions" (NIST, 2013). This is accomplished by the selection and implementation of NIST SP 800-53, Revision 4, described security controls. (See Figure 4 below). They are organized into eighteen families to address sub-set security areas such as access control, physical security, incident response, etc. The use of these controls is typically tailored to the security categorization by the respective system owner relying upon FIPS 199 categorization standards. A higher security categorization requires the greater implementation of these controls.

ID	FAMILY	ID	FAMILY
AC	Access Control	MP	Media Protection
AT	Awareness and Training	PE	Physical and Environmental Protection
AU	Audit and Accountability	PL	Planning
CA	Security Assessment and Authorization	PS	Personnel Security
CM	Configuration Management	RA	Risk Assessment
CP	Contingency Planning	SA	System and Services Acquisition
IA	Identification and Authentication	SC	System and Communications Protection
IR	Incident Response	SI	System and Information Integrity
MA	Maintenance	PM	Program Management

**Note that these are all the control families required within DOD. Under the NIST 800-171 effort, not all control families are used or required.

Figure 4. Security Control Identifiers and Family Names (NIST, 2013)

Security Information and Event Management (SIEM) Solutions

The SIEM tool plays a pivotal role in any viable "First Generation" implementation. Based on NIST and DHS guidance, a capable SIEM appliance must provide the following functionalities:

- "Aggregate data from "across a diverse set" of security tool sources;
- Analyze the multi-source data;
- Engage in explorations of data based on changing needs
- Make quantitative use of data for security (not just reporting) purposes including the development and use of risk scores; and
- Maintain actionable awareness of the changing security situation on a real-time basis" (Levinson, 2011).

"Effectiveness is further enhanced when the output is formatted to provide information that is specific, measurable, actionable, relevant, and timely" (NIST, 2011). The SIEM device is the vital core of a full solution that collects, analyzes, and alerts the cyber-professional of potential and actual dangers in their environment.

Several major SIEM solutions can effectively meet the requirements of NIST SP 800-137. They include products, for example, IBM® Security, Splunk®, and Hewlett Packard's® ArcSight® products.

For example, Logrhythm ® was highly rated in the 2014 SIEM evaluation. Logrhythm® provided network event monitoring and alerts of potential security compromises. The implementation of an enterprise-grade SIEM solution is necessary to meet growing cybersecurity requirements for auditing of security logs and capabilities to respond to cyber-incidents. SIEM products will continue to play a critical and evolving role in the demands for "…increased security and rapid response to events throughout the network" (McAfee® Foundstone Professional Services®, 2013). Improvements and upgrades of SIEM tools are critical to providing a more highly responsive capability for future generations of these appliances in the marketplace.

Next Generations

Future generations of CM would include specific expanded capabilities and functionalities of the SIEM device. These second generation and beyond evolutions would be more effective solutions in future dynamic and hostile network environments. Such advancements might also include increased access to a greater pool of threat database signature repositories or more expansive heuristics that could identify active anomalies within a target network.

Another futuristic capability might include the use of Artificial Intelligence (AI). Improved capabilities of a SIEM appliance with AI augmentation would further enhance human threat analysis and provide for more automated responsiveness. "The concept of predictive analysis involves using statistical methods and decision tools that analyze current and historical data to make predictions about future events…" (SANS Institute). The next generation would boost human response times and abilities to defend against attacks in a matter of milli-seconds vice hours.

Finally, in describing the next generations of CM, it is not only imperative to expand data, informational, and intelligence inputs for new and more capable SIEM products, but that input and corresponding data sets must also be thoroughly vetted for completeness and accuracy. Increased access to signature and heuristic activity-based analysis databases would provide a more significant risk reduction. More substantial support from the private industry and the Intelligence Community would also be significant improvements for Agencies that are continually struggling against a more-capable and better-resourced threat.

CM will not be a reality until vendors and agencies can integrate the right people, processes, and technologies. "Security needs to be positioned as an enabler of the organization—it must take its place alongside human resources, financial resources, sound business processes and strategies, information technology, and intellectual capital as the elements of success for accomplishing the mission," (Caralli, 2004). CM is not just a technical solution. It requires capable organizations with trained personnel, creating effective policies and procedures with the requisite technologies to stay ahead of the growing threats in cyberspace.

Figure 6 below provides a graphic depiction of what CM components are needed to create a holistic NIST SP 800-137-compliant solution; this demonstrates the First-Generation representation. Numerous vendors are describing that they have the "holy grail" solution, but until they can prove they meet this description in total, it is unlikely they have a complete implementation of a thorough CM solution yet.

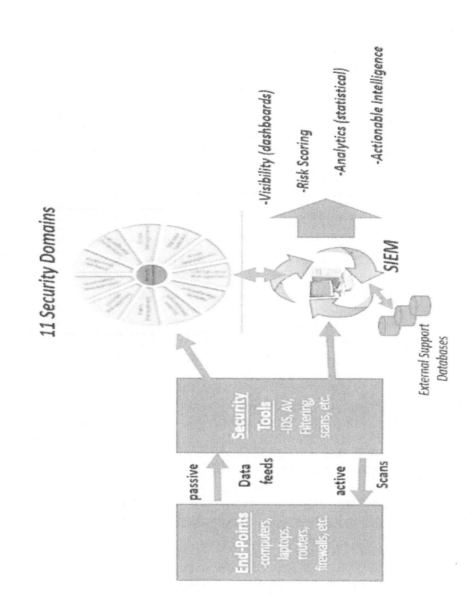

First Generation Continuous Monitoring

Footnotes for "Continuous Monitoring: A More Detailed Discussion"

Balakrishnan, B. (2015, October 6). *Insider Threat Mitigation Guidance.* Retrieved from SANS Institute Infosec Reading Room: https://www.sans.org/reading-room/whitepapers/monitoring/insider-threat-mitigation-guidance-36307

Caralli, R. A. (2004, December). *Managing Enterprise Security (CMU/SEI-2004-TN-046).* Retrieved from Software Engineering Institute: http://www.sei.cmu.edu/reports/04tn046.pdf

Committee on National Security Systems. (2010, April 26). *National Information Assurance (IA) Glossary.* Retrieved from National Counterintelligence & Security Center: http://www.ncsc.gov/nittf/docs/CNSSI-4009_National_Information_Assurance.pdf

Department of Defense. (2014, March 12). *DOD Instructions 8510.01: Risk Management Framework (RMF) for DoD Information Technology (IT).* Retrieved from Defense Technical Information Center (DTIC): http://www.dtic.mil/whs/directives/corres/pdf/851001_2014.pdf

GSA. (2012, January 27). *Continuous Monitoring Strategy & Guide, v1.1.* Retrieved from General Services Administration: http://www.gsa.gov/graphics/staffoffices/Continuous_Monitoring_Strategy_Guide_072712.pdf

Joint Medical Logistics Functional Development Center. (2015). JMLFDC Continuous Monitoring Strategy Plan and Procedure. Ft Detrick, MD.

Kavanagh, K. M., Nicolett, M., & Rochford, O. (2014, June 25). *Magic Quadrant for Security Information and Event Management.* Retrieved from Gartner: http://www.gartner.com/technology/reprints.do?id=1-1W8AO4W&ct=140627&st=sb&mkt_tok=3RkMMJWWfF9wsRolsqrJcO%2FhmjTEU5z17u8IWa%2B0gYkz2EFye%2BLIHETpodcMTcVkNb%2FYDBceEJhqyQJxPr3FKdANz8JpRhnqAA%3D%3D

Kolenko, M. M. (2016, February 18). *SPECIAL-The Human Element of Cybersecurity.* Retrieved from Homeland Security Today.US: http://www.hstoday.us/briefings/industry-news/single-article/special-the-human-element-of-cybersecurity/54008efd46e93863f54db0f7352dde2c.html

Levinson, B. (2011, October). *Federal Cybersecurity Best Practices Study: Information Security Continuous Monitoring.* Retrieved from Center for Regulatory Effectiveness:

http://www.thecre.com/fisma/wp-content/uploads/2011/10/Federal-Cybersecurity-Best-Practice.ISCM_2.pdf

McAfee® Foundstone® Professional Services. (2013). *McAfee.* Retrieved from White Paper: Creating and Maintaining a SOC: http://www.mcafee.com/us/resources/white-papers/foundstone/wp-creating-maintaining-soc.pdf

NIST. (2011-A, August). *NIST SP 800-128: Guide for Security-Focused Configuration Management of Information Systems.* Retrieved from NIST Computer Security Resource Center: http://csrc.nist.gov/publications/nistpubs/800-128/sp800-128.pdf

NIST. (2011-B, September). *Special Publication 800-137: Information Security Continuous Monitoring (ISCM) for Federal Information Systems and Organizations.* Retrieved from NIST Computer Security Resource Center: http://csrc.nist.gov/publications/nistpubs/800-137/SP800-137-Final.pdf

NIST. (2012, January). *NIST Interagency Report 7756: CAESARS Framework Extension: An Enterprise Continuous Monitoring Technical Reference Model (Second Draft).* Retrieved from NIST Computer Resource Security Center: http://csrc.nist.gov/publications/drafts/nistir-7756/Draft-NISTIR-7756_second-public-draft.pdf

NIST. (2013, April). *NIST SP 800-53, Rev 4: Security and Privacy Controls for Federal Information Systems.* Retrieved from NIST: http://nvlpubs.nist.gov/nistpubs/SpecialPublications/NIST.SP.800-53r4.pdf

Ross, R., Katzke, S., & Toth, P. (2005, October 17). *The New FISMA Standards and Guidelines Changing the Dynamic of Information Security for the Federal Government.* Retrieved from Information Technology Promotion Agency of Japan: https://www.ipa.go.jp/files/000015362.pdf

Sann, W. (2016, January 8). *The Key Missing Piece of Your Cyber Strategy? Visibility.* Retrieved from Nextgov: http://www.nextgov.com/technology-news/tech-insider/2016/01/key-missing-element-your-cyber-strategy-visibility/124974/

SANS Institute. (2016, March 6). *Beyond Continuous Monitoring: Threat Modeling for Real-time Response.* Retrieved from SANS Institute: http://www.sans.org/reading-room/whitepapers/analyst/continuous-monitoring-threat-modeling-real-time-response-35185

Sternstein, A. (2015, January 6). *OPM Hackers Skirted Cutting-Edge Intrusion Detection System, Official Says.* Retrieved from Nextgov: http://www.nextgov.com/cybersecurity/2015/06/opm-hackers-skirted-cutting-edge-interior-intrusion-detection-official-says/114649/

APPENDIX D – NIST 800-171 COMPLIANCE CHECKLIST

The following compliance checklist is intended to provide a guide to conduct a "self-assessment" of the company's overall cybersecurity posture as required by NIST 800-171.

*Assessment Method: Refer to NIST 800-171A, **Assessing Security Requirements for Controlled Unclassified Information**, that describes types and means to self-validate the control. The three assessment methods are: examine, interview, and test.

Control #	Description	Assessment Method*	Document (e.g., SSP or Co. Procedure Guide)	Page #	Reviewed By	Validated By
Access Control (AC)						
3.1.1	*Limit information system access to authorized users, processes acting on behalf of authorized users, or devices (including other information systems)*					
3.1.1[a]	Authorized users are identified.					
3.1.1[b]	Processes acting on behalf of authorized users are identified.					
3.1.1[c]	Devices (and other systems) authorized to connect to the system are identified.					
3.1.1[d]	System access is limited to authorized users.					
3.1.1[e]	System access is limited to processes acting on behalf of authorized users.					
3.1.1[f]	System access is limited to authorized devices (including other systems).					
3.1.1[a]	Authorized users are identified.					
3.1.2	*Limit information system access to the types of transactions and functions that authorized users are permitted to execute*					
3.1.2[a]	The types of transactions and functions that authorized users are permitted to execute are defined.					
3.1.2[b]	System access is limited to the defined types of transactions and functions for authorized users.					
3.1.3	*Control the flow of CUI in accordance with approved authorizations*					

3.1.3[a]	Information flow control policies are defined.	
3.1.3[b]	Methods and enforcement mechanisms for controlling the flow of CUI are defined.	
3.1.3[c]	Designated sources and destinations (e.g., networks, individuals, and devices) for CUI within the system and between interconnected systems are identified.	
3.1.3[d]	Authorizations for controlling the flow of CUI are defined.	
3.1.3[e]	Approved authorizations for controlling the flow of CUI are enforced.	
3.1.4	**Separate the duties of individuals to reduce the risk of malevolent activity without collusion**	
3.1.4[a]	The duties of individuals requiring separation are defined.	
3.1.4[b]	Responsibilities for duties that require separation are assigned to separate individuals.	
3.1.4[c]	Access privileges that enable individuals to exercise the duties that require separation are granted to separate individuals.	
3.1.5	**Employ the principle of least privilege, including for specific security functions and privileged accounts**	
3.1.5[a]	Privileged accounts are identified.	
3.1.5[b]	Access to privileged accounts is authorized in accordance with the principle of least privilege.	
3.1.5[c]	Security functions are identified.	
3.1.5[d]	Access to security functions is authorized in accordance with the principle of least privilege.	
3.1.6	**Use non-privileged accounts or roles when accessing nonsecurity functions**	
3.1.6[a]	Nonsecurity functions are identified.	
3.1.6[b]	Users are required to use non-privileged accounts or roles when accessing nonsecurity functions.	

3.1.7	**Prevent non-privileged users from executing privileged functions and audit the execution of such functions**	
3.1.7[a]	Privileged functions are defined.	
3.1.7[b]	Non-privileged users are defined.	
3.1.7[c]	Non-privileged users are prevented from executing privileged functions.	
3.1.7[d]	The execution of privileged functions is captured in audit logs.	
3.1.8	**Limit unsuccessful logon attempts**	
3.1.8[a]	The means of limiting unsuccessful logon attempts is defined.	
3.1.8[b]	The defined means of limiting unsuccessful logon attempts is implemented.	
3.1.9	**Provide privacy and security notices consistent with applicable CUI rules**	
3.1.9[a]	Privacy and security notices required by CUI-specified rules are identified, consistent, and associated with the specific CUI category.	
3.1.9[b]	Privacy and security notices are displayed.	
3.1.10	**Use session lock with pattern-hiding displays to prevent access/viewing of data after period of inactivity**	
3.1.10[a]	The period of inactivity after which the system initiates a session lock is defined.	
3.1.10[b]	Access to the system and viewing of data is prevented by initiating a session lock after the defined period of inactivity.	
3.1.10[c]	Previously visible information is concealed via a pattern-hiding display after the defined period of inactivity.	
3.1.11	**Terminate (automatically) a user session after a defined condition**	
3.1.11[a]	Conditions requiring a user session to terminate are defined.	
3.1.11[b]	A user session is automatically terminated after any of the defined conditions occur.	

Control #		Description	Assessment Method*	Document (e.g., SSP or Co. Procedure Guide)	Page #	Reviewed By	Validated By
Access Control (AC)							
3.1.12		*Monitor and control remote access sessions*					
3.1.12[a]		*Remote access sessions are permitted.*					
3.1.12[b]		*The types of permitted remote access are identified.*					
3.1.12[c]		*Remote access sessions are controlled.*					
3.1.12[d]		*Remote access sessions are monitored.*					
3.1.13		*Employ cryptographic mechanisms to protect the confidentiality of remote access sessions*					
3.1.13[a]		*Cryptographic mechanisms to protect the confidentiality of remote access sessions are identified.*					
3.1.13[b]		*Cryptographic mechanisms to protect the confidentiality of remote access sessions are implemented.*					
3.1.14		*Route remote access via managed access control points*					
3.1.14[a]		*Managed access control points are identified and implemented.*					
3.1.14[b]		*Remote access is routed through managed network access control points.*					
3.1.15		*Authorize remote execution of privileged commands and remote access to security-relevant information*					
3.1.15[a]		*Privileged commands authorized for remote execution are identified.*					
3.1.15[b]		*Security-relevant information authorized to be accessed remotely is identified.*					
3.1.15[c]		*The execution of the identified privileged commands via remote access is authorized.*					

3.1.15[d]	*Access to the identified security-relevant information via remote access is authorized.*	
3.1.16	**Authorize wireless access prior to allowing such connections**	
3.1.16[a]	*Wireless access points are identified.*	
3.1.16[b]	*Wireless access is authorized prior to allowing such connections.*	
3.1.17	**Protect wireless access using authentication and encryption**	
3.1.17[a]	*Wireless access to the system is protected using authentication.*	
3.1.17[b]	*Wireless access to the system is protected using encryption.*	
3.1.18	**Control connection of mobile devices**	
3.1.18[a]	*Mobile devices that process, store, or transmit CUI are identified.*	
3.1.18[b]	*Mobile device connections are authorized.*	
3.1.18[c]	*Mobile device connections are monitored and logged.*	
3.1.19	**Encrypt CUI on mobile devices**	
3.1.19[a]	*Mobile devices and mobile computing platforms that process, store, or transmit CUI are identified.*	
3.1.19[b]	*Encryption is employed to protect CUI on identified mobile devices and mobile computing platforms.*	
3.1.20[a]	*Connections to external systems are identified.*	
3.1.20[b]	*The use of external systems is identified.*	
3.1.20[c]	*Connections to external systems are verified.*	
3.1.20[d]	*The use of external systems is verified.*	
3.1.20[e]	*Connections to external systems are controlled/limited.*	
3.1.20[f]	*The use of external systems is controlled/limited.*	
3.1.20[a]	*Connections to external systems are identified.*	
3.1.21	**Limit use of organizational portable storage devices on external systems**	

3.1.21[a]	The use of portable storage devices containing CUI on external systems is identified and documented.	
3.1.21[b]	Limits on the use of portable storage devices containing CUI on external systems are defined.	
3.1.21[c]	The use of portable storage devices containing CUI on external systems is limited as defined.	
3.1.22	**Control CUI posted or processed on publicly accessible systems**	
3.1.22[a]	Individuals authorized to post or process information on publicly accessible systems are identified.	
3.1.22[b]	Procedures to ensure CUI is not posted or processed on publicly accessible systems are identified.	
3.1.22[c]	A review process is in place prior to posting of any content to publicly accessible systems.	
3.1.22[d]	Content on publicly accessible systems is reviewed to ensure that it does not include CUI.	
3.1.22[e]	Mechanisms are in place to remove and address improper posting of CUI.	
3.1.22[a]	Individuals authorized to post or process information on publicly accessible systems are identified.	

Control #	Description	Assessment Method*	Document (e.g., SSP or Co. Procedure Guide)	Page #	Reviewed By	Validated By
Awareness & Training (AT)						
3.2.1	**Ensure that managers, systems administrators, and users of organizational information systems are made aware of the security risks associated with their activities and of the applicable policies, standards, and procedures related to the security of organizational information systems**					
3.2.1[a]	Security risks associated with organizational activities involving CUI are identified.					
3.2.1[b]	Policies, standards, and procedures related to the security of the system are identified.					
3.2.1[c]	Managers, systems administrators, and users of the system are made aware of the security risks associated with their activities.					
3.2.1[d]	Managers, systems administrators, and users of the system are made aware of the applicable policies, standards, and procedures related to the security of the system.					
3.2.2	**Ensure that organizational personnel are adequately trained to carry out their assigned information security-related duties and responsibilities**					
3.2.2[a]	Information security-related duties, roles, and responsibilities are defined.					
3.2.2[b]	Information security-related duties, roles, and responsibilities are assigned to designated personnel.					
3.2.2[c]	Personnel are adequately trained to carry out their assigned information					

		security-related duties, roles, and responsibilities.
3.2.3		**Provide security awareness training on recognizing and reporting potential indicators of insider threat**
3.2.3[a]		*Potential indicators associated with insider threats are identified.*
3.2.3[b]		*Security awareness training on recognizing and reporting potential indicators of insider threat is provided to managers and employees.*

Control #	Description	Assessment Method*	Document (e.g., SSP or Co. Procedure Guide)	Page #	Reviewed By	Validated By
Audit & Accountability (AU)						
3.3.1	*Create, protect, and retain information system audit records to the extent needed to enable the monitoring, analysis, investigation, and reporting of unlawful, unauthorized, or inappropriate information system activity*					
3.3.1[a]	*Audit logs needed (i.e., event types to be logged) to enable the monitoring, analysis, investigation, and reporting of unlawful or unauthorized system activity are specified.*					
3.3.1[b]	*The content of audit records needed to support monitoring, analysis, investigation, and reporting of unlawful or unauthorized system activity is defined.*					
3.3.1[c]	*Audit records are created (generated).*					
3.3.1[d]	*Audit records, once created, contain the defined content.*					
3.3.1[e]	*Retention requirements for audit records are defined.*					
3.3.1[f]	*Audit records are retained as defined.*					
3.3.2	*Ensure that the actions of individual information system users can be uniquely traced to those users, so they can be held accountable for their actions*					
3.3.2[a]	*The content of the audit records needed to support the ability to uniquely trace users to their actions is defined.*					
3.3.2[b]	*Audit records, once created, contain the defined content.*					

3.3.3	**Review and update audited events**	
3.3.3[a]	A process for determining when to review logged events is defined.	
3.3.3[b]	Event types being logged are reviewed in accordance with the defined review process.	
3.3.3[c]	Event types being logged are updated based on the review.	
3.3.4	**Alert in the event of an audit process failure**	
3.3.4[a]	Personnel or roles to be alerted in the event of an audit logging process failure are identified.	
3.3.4[b]	Types of audit logging process failures for which alert will be generated are defined.	
3.3.4[c]	Identified personnel or roles are alerted in the event of an audit logging process failure.	
3.3.5	**Correlate audit review, analysis, and reporting processes for investigation and response to indications of inappropriate, suspicious, or unusual activity**	
3.3.5[a]	Audit record review, analysis, and reporting processes for investigation and response to indications of unlawful, unauthorized, suspicious, or unusual activity are defined.	
3.3.5[b]	Defined audit record review, analysis, and reporting processes are correlated.	
3.3.6	**Provide audit reduction and report generation to support on-demand analysis and reporting**	
3.3.6[a]	An audit record reduction capability that supports on-demand analysis is provided.	
3.3.6[b]	A report generation capability that supports on-demand reporting is provided.	
3.3.7	**Provide an information system capability that compares and**	

	synchronizes internal system clocks with an authoritative source to generate time stamps for audit records	
3.3.7[a]	*Internal system clocks are used to generate time stamps for audit records.*	
3.3.7[b]	*An authoritative source with which to compare and synchronize internal system clocks is specified.*	
3.3.7[c]	*Internal system clocks used to generate time stamps for audit records are compared to and synchronized with the specified authoritative time source.*	
3.3.8	***Protect audit information and audit tools from unauthorized access, modification, and deletion***	
3.3.8[a]	*Audit information is protected from unauthorized access.*	
3.3.8[b]	*Audit information is protected from unauthorized modification.*	
3.3.8[c]	*Audit information is protected from unauthorized deletion.*	
3.3.8[d]	*Audit logging tools are protected from unauthorized access.*	
3.3.8[e]	*Audit logging tools are protected from unauthorized modification.*	
3.3.8[f]	*Audit logging tools are protected from unauthorized deletion.*	
3.3.9	***Limit management of audit functionality to a subset of privileged users***	
3.3.9[a]	*A subset of privileged users granted access to manage audit logging functionality is defined.*	
3.3.9[b]	*Management of audit logging functionality is limited to the defined subset of privileged users.*	

Control #	Description	Assessment Method*	Document (e.g., SSP or Co. Procedure Guide)	Page #	Reviewed By	Validated By
Configuration Management (CM)						
3.4.1	*Establish and maintain baseline configurations and inventories of organizational information systems (including hardware, software, firmware, and documentation) throughout the respective system development life cycles*					
3.4.1[a]	A baseline configuration is established.					
3.4.1[b]	The baseline configuration includes hardware, software, firmware, and documentation.					
3.4.1[c]	The baseline configuration is maintained (reviewed and updated) throughout the system development life cycle.					
3.4.1[d]	A system inventory is established.					
3.4.1[e]	The system inventory includes hardware, software, firmware, and documentation.					
3.4.1[f]	The inventory is maintained (reviewed and updated) throughout the system development life cycle.					
3.4.2	*Establish and enforce security configuration settings for information technology products employed in organizational information systems*					
3.4.2[a]	Security configuration settings for information technology products employed in the system are established and included in the baseline configuration.					
3.4.2[b]	Security configuration settings for information technology products employed in the system are enforced.					

3.4.3		*Track, review, approve/disapprove, and audit changes to information systems*
3.4.3[a]		*Changes to the system are tracked.*
3.4.3[b]		*Changes to the system are reviewed.*
3.4.3[c]		*Changes to the system are approved or disapproved.*
3.4.3[d]		*Changes to the system are logged.*
3.4.4		*Analyze the security impact of changes prior to implementation*
3.4.5		*Define, document, approve, and enforce physical and logical access restrictions associated with changes to the information system*
3.4.5[a]		*Physical access restrictions associated with changes to the system are defined.*
3.4.5[b]		*Physical access restrictions associated with changes to the system are documented.*
3.4.5[c]		*Physical access restrictions associated with changes to the system are approved.*
3.4.5[d]		*Physical access restrictions associated with changes to the system are enforced.*
3.4.5[e]		*Logical access restrictions associated with changes to the system are defined.*
3.4.5[f]		*Logical access restrictions associated with changes to the system are documented.*
3.4.5[g]		*Logical access restrictions associated with changes to the system are approved.*
3.4.5[h]		*Logical access restrictions associated with changes to the system are enforced.*
3.4.6		*Employ the principle of least functionality by configuring the information system to provide only essential capabilities*

3.4.6[a]	Essential system capabilities are defined based on the principle of least functionality.	
3.4.6[b]	The system is configured to provide only the defined essential capabilities.	
3.4.7	**Restrict, disable, and prevent the use of nonessential programs, functions, ports, protocols, and services**	
3.4.7[a]	Essential programs are defined.	
3.4.7[b]	The use of nonessential programs is defined.	
3.4.7[c]	The use of nonessential programs is restricted, disabled, or prevented as defined.	
3.4.7[d]	Essential functions are defined.	
3.4.7[e]	The use of nonessential functions is defined.	
3.4.7[f]	The use of nonessential functions is restricted, disabled, or prevented as defined.	
3.4.7[g]	Essential ports are defined.	
3.4.7[h]	The use of nonessential ports is defined.	
3.4.7[i]	The use of nonessential ports is restricted, disabled, or prevented as defined.	
3.4.7[j]	Essential protocols are defined.	
3.4.7[k]	The use of nonessential protocols is defined.	
3.4.7[l]	The use of nonessential protocols is restricted, disabled, or prevented as defined.	
3.4.7[m]	Essential services are defined.	
3.4.7[n]	The use of nonessential services is defined.	
3.4.7[o]	The use of nonessential services is restricted, disabled, or prevented as defined.	
3.4.8	**Apply deny-by-exception (blacklist) policy to prevent the use of unauthorized software or deny all, permit-by-exception**	

	(whitelisting) policy to allow the execution of authorized software	
3.4.8[a]	A policy specifying whether whitelisting or blacklisting is to be implemented is specified.	
3.4.8[b]	The software allowed to execute under whitelisting or denied use under blacklisting is specified.	
3.4.8[c]	Whitelisting to allow the execution of authorized software or blacklisting to prevent the use of unauthorized software is implemented as specified.	
3.4.9	**Control and monitor user-installed software**	
3.4.9[a]	A policy for controlling the installation of software by users is established.	
3.4.9[b]	Installation of software by users is controlled based on the established policy.	
3.4.9[c]	Installation of software by users is monitored.	

Control #	Description	Assessment Method*	Document (e.g., SSP or Co. Procedure Guide)	Page #	Reviewed By	Validated By
Identification & Authentication (IA)						
3.5.1	**Identify information system users, processes acting on behalf of users, or devices**					
3.5.1[a]	System users are identified.					
3.5.1[b]	Processes acting on behalf of users are identified.					
3.5.1[c]	Devices accessing the system are identified.					
3.5.2	**Authenticate (or verify) the identities of those users, processes, or devices, as a prerequisite to allowing access to organizational information systems**					
3.5.2[a]	The identity of each user is authenticated or verified as a prerequisite to system access.					
3.5.2[b]	The identity of each process acting on behalf of a user is authenticated or verified as a prerequisite to system access.					
3.5.2[c]	The identity of each device accessing or connecting to the system is authenticated or verified as a prerequisite to system access.					
3.5.3	**Use multifactor authentication for local and network access to privileged accounts and for network access to non-privileged accounts**					
3.5.3[a]	Privileged accounts are identified.					
3.5.3[b]	Multifactor authentication is implemented for local access to privileged accounts.					
3.5.3[c]	Multifactor authentication is implemented for network access to privileged accounts.					

3.5.3[d]	Multifactor authentication is implemented for network access to non-privileged accounts.	
3.5.4	**Employ replay-resistant authentication mechanisms for network access to privileged and nonprivileged accounts**	
3.5.5	**Prevent reuse of identifiers for a defined period**	
3.5.5[a]	A period within which identifiers cannot be reused is defined.	
3.5.5[b]	Reuse of identifiers is prevented within the defined period.	
3.5.6	**Disable identifiers after a defined period of inactivity**	
3.5.6[a]	A period of inactivity, after which an identifier is disabled is defined.	
3.5.6[b]	Identifiers are disabled after the defined period of inactivity.	
3.5.7	**Enforce a minimum password complexity and change of characters when new passwords are created**	
3.5.7[a]	Password complexity requirements are defined.	
3.5.7[b]	Password change of character requirements are defined.	
3.5.7[c]	Minimum password complexity requirements as defined are enforced when new passwords are created.	
3.5.7[d]	Minimum password change of character requirements as defined are enforced when new passwords are created.	
3.5.8	**Prohibit password reuse for a specified number of generations**	
3.5.8[a]	The number of generations during which a password cannot be reused is specified.	
3.5.8[b]	Reuse of passwords is prohibited during the specified number of generations.	
3.5.9	**Allow temporary password use for system logons with an**	

	immediate change to a permanent password	
3.5.10	***Store and transmit only encrypted representation of passwords***	
3.5.10[a]	*Passwords are cryptographically protected in storage.*	
3.5.10[b]	*Passwords are cryptographically protected in transit.*	
3.5.11.	***Obscure feedback of authentication information***	

Control #	Description	Assessment Method*	Document (e.g., SSP or Co. Procedure Guide)	Page #	Reviewed By	Validated By
Incident Response (IR)						
3.6.1	*Establish an operational incident-handling capability for organizational information systems that includes adequate preparation, detection, analysis, containment, recovery, and user response activities*					
3.6.1[a]	*An operational incident-handling capability is established.*					
3.6.1[b]	*The operational incident-handling capability includes preparation.*					
3.6.1[c]	*The operational incident-handling capability includes detection.*					
3.6.1[d]	*The operational incident-handling capability includes analysis.*					
3.6.1[e]	*The operational incident-handling capability includes containment.*					
3.6.1[f]	*The operational incident-handling capability includes recovery.*					
3.6.1[g]	*The operational incident-handling capability includes user response activities.*					
3.6.2	*Track, document, and report incidents to appropriate officials and/or authorities both internal and external to the organization*					
3.6.2[a]	*Incidents are tracked.*					
3.6.2[b]	*Incidents are documented.*					
3.6.2[c]	*Authorities to whom incidents are to be reported are identified.*					
3.6.2[d]	*Organizational officials to whom incidents are to be reported are identified.*					
3.6.2[e]	*Identified authorities are notified of incidents.*					
3.6.2[f]	*Identified organizational officials are notified of incidents.*					

3.6.3　Test the organizational incident response capability

Control #	Description	Assessment Method*	Document (e.g., SSP or Co. Procedure Guide)	Page #	Reviewed By	Validated By
Maintenance (MA)						
3.7.1	Perform maintenance on organizational information systems					
3.7.2	Provide effective controls on the tools, techniques, mechanisms, and personnel used to conduct information system maintenance					
3.7.2[a]	Tools used to conduct system maintenance are controlled.					
3.7.2[b]	Techniques used to conduct system maintenance are controlled.					
3.7.2[c]	Mechanisms used to conduct system maintenance are controlled.					
3.7.2[d]	Personnel used to conduct system maintenance are controlled.					
3.7.3	Ensure equipment removed for off-site maintenance is sanitized of any CUI					
3.7.4	Check media containing diagnostic and test programs for malicious code before the media are used in the information system					
3.7.5	Require multifactor authentication to establish nonlocal maintenance sessions via external network connections and terminate such connections when nonlocal maintenance is complete					
3.7.5[a]	Multifactor authentication is used to establish nonlocal maintenance sessions via external network connections.					

3.7.5[b]	*Nonlocal maintenance sessions established via external network connections are terminated when nonlocal maintenance is complete.*	
3.7.6	***Supervise the maintenance activities of maintenance personnel without required access authorization***	

Control #	Description	Assessment Method*	Document (e.g., SSP or Co. Procedure Guide)	Page #	Reviewed By	Validated By
Media Protection (MP)						
3.8.1	*Protect (i.e., physically control and securely store) information system media containing CUI, both paper and digital*					
3.8.1[a]	*Paper media containing CUI is physically controlled.*					
3.8.1[b]	*Digital media containing CUI is physically controlled.*					
3.8.1[c]	*Paper media containing CUI is securely stored.*					
3.8.1[d]	*Digital media containing CUI is securely stored.*					
3.8.2	*Limit access to CUI on information system media to authorized users*					
3.8.3	*Sanitize or destroy information system media containing CUI before disposal or release for reuse*					
3.8.3[a]	*System media containing CUI is sanitized or destroyed before disposal.*					
3.8.3[b]	*System media containing CUI is sanitized before it is released for reuse.*					
3.8.4	*Mark media with necessary CUI markings and distribution limitations*					
3.8.4[a]	*Media containing CUI is marked with applicable CUI markings.*					
3.8.4[b]	*Media containing CUI is marked with distribution limitations.*					
3.8.5	*Control access to media containing CUI and maintain accountability for media during transport outside of controlled areas*					
3.8.5[a]	*Access to media containing CUI is controlled.*					

3.8.5[b]	*Accountability for media containing CUI is maintained during transport outside of controlled areas.*	
3.8.6	*Implement cryptographic mechanisms to protect the confidentiality of CUI stored on digital media during transport unless otherwise protected by alternative physical safeguards*	
3.8.7	*Control the use of removable media on information system components*	
3.8.8	*Prohibit the use of portable storage devices when such devices have no identifiable owner*	
3.8.9	*Protect the confidentiality of backup CUI at storage locations*	

Control #	Description	Assessment Method*	Document (e.g., SSP or Co. Procedure Guide)	Page #	Reviewed By	Validated By
Personnel Security (PS)						
3.9.1	*Screen individuals prior to authorizing access to information systems containing CUI*					
3.9.2	*Ensure that CUI and information systems containing CUI are protected during and after personnel actions such as terminations and transfers*					
3.9.2[a]	*A policy and/or process for terminating system access and any credentials coincident with personnel actions is established.*					
3.9.2[b]	*System access and credentials are terminated consistent with personnel actions such as termination or transfer.*					
3.9.2[c]	*The system is protected during and after personnel transfer actions.*					

Control #	Description	Assessment Method*	Document (e.g., SSP or Co. Procedure Guide)	Page #	Reviewed By	Validated By
Physical Security (PP)						
3.10.1	*Limit physical access to organizational information systems, equipment, and the respective operating environments to authorized individuals*					
3.10.1[a]	Authorized individuals allowed physical access are identified.					
3.10.1[b]	Physical access to organizational systems is limited to authorized individuals.					
3.10.1[c]	Physical access to equipment is limited to authorized individuals.					
3.10.1[d]	Physical access to operating environments is limited to authorized individuals.					
3.10.2	*Protect and monitor the physical facility and support infrastructure for those information systems*					
3.10.2[a]	The physical facility where organizational systems reside is protected.					
3.10.2[b]	The support infrastructure for organizational systems is protected.					
3.10.2[c]	The physical facility where organizational systems reside is monitored.					
3.10.2[d]	The support infrastructure for organizational systems is monitored.					
3.10.3	*Escort visitors and monitor visitor activity*					
3.10.3[a]	Visitors are escorted.					
3.10.3[b]	Visitor activity is monitored.					
3.10.4	*Maintain audit logs of physical access*					

3.10.5	**Control and manage physical access devices**	
3.10.5[a]	Physical access devices are identified.	
3.10.5[b]	Physical access devices are controlled.	
3.10.5[c]	Physical access devices are managed.	
3.10.6	**Enforce safeguarding measures for CUI at alternate worksites (e.g., telework sites)**	
3.10.6[a]	Safeguarding measures for CUI are defined for alternate work sites.	
3.10.6[b]	Safeguarding measures for CUI are enforced for alternate work sites.	

Control #	Description	Assessment Method*	Document (e.g., SSP or Co. Procedure Guide)	Page #	Reviewed By	Validated By
Risk Assessments (RA)						
3.11.1	*Periodically assess the risk to organizational operations (including mission, functions, image, or reputation), organizational assets, and individuals, resulting from the operation of organizational information systems and the associated processing, storage, or transmission of CUI*					
3.11.1[a]	*The frequency to assess risk to organizational operations, organizational assets, and individuals is defined.*					
3.11.1[b]	*Risk to organizational operations, organizational assets, and individuals resulting from the operation of an organizational system that processes, stores, or transmits CUI is assessed with the defined frequency.*					
3.11.2	*Scan for vulnerabilities in the information system and applications periodically and when new vulnerabilities affecting the system are identified*					
3.11.2[a]	*The frequency to scan for vulnerabilities in organizational systems and applications is defined.*					
3.11.2[b]	*Vulnerability scans are performed on organizational systems with the defined frequency.*					
3.11.2[c]	*Vulnerability scans are performed on applications with the defined frequency.*					

3.11.2[d]	*Vulnerability scans are performed on organizational systems when new vulnerabilities are identified.*	
3.11.2[e]	*Vulnerability scans are performed on applications when new vulnerabilities are identified.*	
3.11.3	**Remediate vulnerabilities in accordance with assessments of risk**	
3.11.3[a]	*Vulnerabilities are identified.*	
3.11.3[b]	*Vulnerabilities are remediated in accordance with risk assessments.*	

Control #	Description	Assessment Method*	Document (e.g., SSP or Co. Procedure Guide)	Page #	Reviewed By	Validated By
Security Assessments (SA)						
3.12.1	Periodically assess the security controls in organizational information systems to determine if the controls are effective in their application					
3.12.1[a]	The frequency of security control assessments is defined.					
3.12.1[b]	Security controls are assessed with the defined frequency to determine if the controls are effective in their application.					
3.12.2	Develop and implement plans of action designed to correct deficiencies and reduce or eliminate vulnerabilities in organizational information systems					
3.12.2[a]	Deficiencies and vulnerabilities to be addressed by the plan of action are identified.					
3.12.2[b]	A plan of action is developed to correct identified deficiencies and reduce or eliminate identified vulnerabilities.					
3.12.2[c]	The plan of action is implemented to correct identified deficiencies and reduce or eliminate identified vulnerabilities.					
3.12.3	Monitor information system security controls on an ongoing basis to ensure the continued effectiveness of the controls					
3.12.4	Develop, document, and periodically update system security plans that describe system boundaries, system environments of operation, how security requirements are implemented, and the					

	relationships with or connections to other systems	
3.12.4[a]	A system security plan is developed.	
3.12.4[b]	The system boundary is described and documented in the system security plan.	
3.12.4[c]	The system environment of operation is described and documented in the system security plan.	
3.12.4[d]	The security requirements identified and approved by the designated authority as non-applicable are identified.	
3.12.4[e]	The method of security requirement implementation is described and documented in the system security plan.	
3.12.4[f]	The relationship with or connection to other systems is described and documented in the system security plan.	
3.12.4[g]	The frequency to update the system security plan is defined.	
3.12.4[h]	System security plan is updated with the defined frequency.	

Control #	Description	Assessment Method*	Document (e.g., SSP or Co. Procedure Guide)	Page #	Reviewed By	Validated By
System & Communications Protection (SC)						
3.13.1	*Monitor, control, and protect organizational communications (i.e., information transmitted or received by organizational information systems) at the external boundaries and key internal boundaries of the information systems*					
3.13.1[a]	*The external system boundary is defined.*					
3.13.1[b]	*Key internal system boundaries are defined.*					
3.13.1[c]	*Communications are monitored at the external system boundary.*					
3.13.1[d]	*Communications are monitored at key internal boundaries.*					
3.13.1[e]	*Communications are controlled at the external system boundary.*					
3.13.1[f]	*Communications are controlled at key internal boundaries.*					
3.13.1[g]	*Communications are protected at the external system boundary.*					
3.13.1[h]	*Communications are protected at key internal boundaries.*					
3.13.2	*Employ architectural designs, software development techniques, and systems engineering principles that promote effective information security within organizational information systems*					
3.13.2[a]	*Architectural designs that promote effective information security are identified.*					
3.13.2[b]	*Software development techniques that promote*					

	effective information security are identified.	
3.13.2[c]	*Systems engineering principles that promote effective information security are identified.*	
3.13.2[d]	*Identified architectural designs that promote effective information security are employed.*	
3.13.2[e]	*Identified software development techniques that promote effective information security are employed.*	
3.13.2[f]	*Identified systems engineering principles that promote effective information security are employed.*	
3.13.3	**Separate user functionality from information system management functionality**	
3.13.3[a]	*User functionality is identified.*	
3.13.3[b]	*System management functionality is identified.*	
3.13.3[c]	*User functionality is separated from system management functionality.*	
3.13.4	**Prevent unauthorized and unintended information transfer via shared system resources**	
3.13.5	**Implement subnetworks for publicly accessible system components that are physically or logically separated from internal networks**	
3.13.5[a]	*Publicly accessible system components are identified.*	
3.13.5[b]	*Subnetworks for publicly accessible system components are physically or logically separated from internal networks.*	
3.13.6	**Deny network communications traffic by default and allow network communications traffic**	

	by exception (i.e., deny all, permit by exception)
3.13.6[a]	Network communications traffic is denied by default.
3.13.6[b]	Network communications traffic is allowed by exception.
3.13.7	Prevent remote devices from simultaneously establishing non-remote connections with the information system and communicating via some other connection to resources in external networks

Control #	Description	Assessment Method*	Document (e.g., SSP or Co. Procedure Guide)	Page #	Reviewed By	Validated By
System & Communications Protection (SC)						
3.13.8	*Implement cryptographic mechanisms to prevent unauthorized disclosure of CUI during transmission unless otherwise protected by alternative physical safeguards*					
3.13.8[a]	*Cryptographic mechanisms intended to prevent unauthorized disclosure of CUI are identified.*					
3.13.8[b]	*Alternative physical safeguards intended to prevent unauthorized disclosure of CUI are identified.*					
3.13.8[c]	*Either cryptographic mechanisms or alternative physical safeguards are implemented to prevent unauthorized disclosure of CUI during transmission.*					
3.13.9	*Terminate network connections associated with communications sessions at the end of the sessions or after a defined period of inactivity*					
3.13.9[a]	*A period of inactivity to terminate network connections associated with communications sessions is defined.*					
3.13.9[b]	*Network connections associated with communications sessions are terminated at the end of the sessions.*					
3.13.9[c]	*Network connections associated with communications sessions are terminated after the defined period of inactivity.*					
3.13.10	*Establish and manage cryptographic keys for*					

		cryptography employed in the information system
3.13.10[a]		Cryptographic keys are established whenever cryptography is employed.
3.13.10[b]		Cryptographic keys are managed whenever cryptography is employed.
3.13.11		**Employ FIPS-validated cryptography when used to protect the confidentiality of CUI**
3.13.12		**Prohibit remote activation of collaborative computing devices and provide indication of devices in use to users present at the device**
3.13.12[a]		Collaborative computing devices are identified.
3.13.12[b]		Collaborative computing devices provide indication to users of devices in use.
3.13.12[c]		Remote activation of collaborative computing devices is prohibited.
3.13.13		**Control and monitor the use of mobile code**
3.13.13[a]		Use of mobile code is controlled.
3.13.13[b]		Use of mobile code is monitored.
3.13.14		**Control and monitor the use of Voice over Internet Protocol (VoIP) technologies**
3.13.14[a]		Use of Voice over Internet Protocol (VoIP) technologies is controlled.
3.13.14[b]		Use of Voice over Internet Protocol (VoIP) technologies is monitored.
3.13.15		**Protect the authenticity of communications sessions**
3.13.16		**Protect the confidentiality of CUI at rest**

Control #	Description	Assessment Method*	Document	Page #	Reviewed By	Validated By
System & Information Integrity (SI)						
3.14.1	*Identify, report, and correct information and information system flaws in a timely manner*					
3.14.1[a]	*The time within which to identify system flaws is specified.*					
3.14.1[b]	*System flaws are identified within the specified time frame.*					
3.14.1[c]	*The time within which to report system flaws is specified.*					
3.14.1[d]	*System flaws are reported within the specified time frame.*					
3.14.1[e]	*The time within which to correct system flaws is specified.*					
3.14.1[f]	*System flaws are corrected within the specified time frame.*					
3.14.2	*Provide protection from malicious code at appropriate locations within organizational information systems*					
3.14.2[a]	*Designated locations for malicious code protection are identified.*					
3.14.2[b]	*Protection from malicious code at designated locations is provided.*					
3.14.3	*Monitor information system security alerts and advisories and take appropriate actions in response*					
3.14.3[a]	*Response actions to system security alerts and advisories are identified.*					
3.14.3[b]	*System security alerts and advisories are monitored.*					
3.14.3[c]	*Actions in response to system security alerts and advisories are taken.*					
3.14.4	*Update malicious code protection mechanisms when new releases are available*					

3.14.5	*Perform periodic scans of the information system and real-time scans of files from external sources as files are downloaded, opened, or executed*	
3.14.5[a]	*The frequency for malicious code scans is defined.*	
3.14.5[b]	*Malicious code scans are performed with the defined frequency.*	
3.14.5[c]	*Real-time malicious code scans of files from external sources as files are downloaded, opened, or executed are performed.*	
3.14.6	*Monitor the information system including inbound and outbound communications traffic, to detect attacks and indicators of potential attacks*	
3.14.6[a]	*The system is monitored to detect attacks and indicators of potential attacks.*	
3.14.6[b]	*Inbound communications traffic is monitored to detect attacks and indicators of potential attacks.*	
3.14.6[c]	*Outbound communications traffic is monitored to detect attacks and indicators of potential attacks.*	
3.14.7	*Identify unauthorized use of the information system*	
3.14.7[a]	*Authorized use of the system is defined.*	
3.14.7[b]	*Unauthorized use of the system is identified.*	

ABOUT THE AUTHOR

Mr. Russo is the former Senior Information Security Engineer within the Department of Defense's (DOD) F-35 Joint Strike Fighter program. He has an extensive background in cybersecurity and is an expert in the Risk Management Framework (RMF) and DOD Instruction 8510, which implements RMF throughout the DOD and the federal government. He holds both a Certified Information Systems Security Professional (CISSP) certification and a CISSP in information security architecture (ISSAP). He holds a 2017 certification as a Chief Information Security Officer (CISO) from the National Defense University, Washington, DC. He retired from the US Army Reserves in 2012 as the Senior Intelligence Officer.

He is the former CISO at the Department of Education, wherein 2016; he led the effort to close over 95% of the outstanding US Congressional and Inspector General cybersecurity shortfall weaknesses spanning as far back as five years.

Mr. Russo is the former Senior Cybersecurity Engineer supporting the Joint Medical Logistics Development Functional Center of the Defense Health Agency (DHA) at Fort Detrick, MD. He led a team of engineering and cybersecurity professionals protecting five major Medical Logistics systems supporting over 200 DOD Medical Treatment Facilities around the globe.

In 2011, Mr. Russo was certified by the Office of Personnel Management as a graduate of the Senior Executive Service Candidate program.

From 2009 through 2011, Mr. Russo was the Chief Technology Officer at the Small Business Administration (SBA). He led a team of over 100 IT professionals in supporting an intercontinental Enterprise IT infrastructure and security operations spanning 12-time zones; he deployed cutting-edge technologies to enhance SBA's business and information sharing operations supporting the small business community. Mr. Russo was the first-ever Program Executive Officer (PEO)/Senior Program Manager in the Office of Intelligence & Analysis at Headquarters, Department of Homeland Security (DHS), Washington, DC. Mr. Russo was responsible for the development and deployment of secure Information and Intelligence support systems for OI&A to include software applications and systems to enhance the DHS mission. He was responsible for the program management development lifecycle during his tenure at DHS.

He holds a Master of Science from the National Defense University in Government Information Leadership with a concentration in Cybersecurity and a Bachelor of Arts in Political Science with a minor in Russian Studies from Lehigh University. He holds Level III Defense Acquisition certification in Program Management, Information Technology, and Systems Engineering. He has been a member of the DOD Acquisition Corps since 2001.

Copyright 2020, Syber-Risk.com, All Rights Reserved
Washington, DC ∞ Tucson, AZ

Made in the USA
Monee, IL
19 January 2022